THE MIDNIGHT COOKBOOK

Thomas Mario

Food and Drink Editor of *Playboy*

COWLES BOOK COMPANY, INC.
A Subsidiary of Henry Regnery Company

Published by Cowles Book Company, Inc.

A subsidiary of Henry Regnery Company

114 West Illinois Street, Chicago, Illinois 60610

Manufactured in the United States of America

SBN 402–50061–X

Library of Congress Catalog Card Number: 76–142115

Contents

Introduction

THE NATURAL HISTORY of the midnight supper begins with teen-agers. By the time young kitchen cossacks of both sexes have reached their college years, they're well schooled in the nightly arts of tearing the remainder of the garlic bread from its moorings, denuding the roast prime ribs of every trace of beef, wantonly sluicing down the balance of the Médoc before its age can be noted, much less discussed.

Late-night suppers are the most favorable time possible for bachelors to display their art in handling the saucepan, the chafing dish, and the salad bowl. Unlike a pompous seven-course dinner, a midnight supper is not just one way to a woman's heart but a shortcut thereto. A diversion like crepes with clams, for instance, prepared at a bachelor's leisure and stashed in his refrigerator until the most propitious moment, takes a mere twenty minutes in the oven to be ready for eating. His girl friend can reverse the coup in even less time by serving something like cold shrimp and artichoke hearts in a creamy dressing, assembled well in advance and kept chilled until the bewitching hour when she decides her shrimp would be most passionately appreciated. Many a girl now clearly realizes that the best overture to a wedding march is the drum roll of a wire whisk beating the eggs for a trimphant *frittata* at midnight. But whether lovers meet and dine *intime* or in a crowd of couples, the twelve o'clock meal is the top round of their evening's pleasures.

Midnight is also the best possible moment for resting one's oars. It's the hour when tension automatically shuts down, when the only sound is the faint hiss and the only fragrance the delicate whiff of foaming butter in the saucepan waiting for the scrambled eggs. There are countless men and women who for the sake of their serenity would, if they could, eat all three meals at midnight.

As a means of entertainment, the midnight supper is rather like an off-Broadway show. It can be staged in the living room, playroom, dining room, terrace, patio, or even the kitchen itself. It's less elaborate and less expensive to mount than a dinner for invited guests. Like music, it joyfully crosses and crisscrosses national boundaries. Its menu is always unpretentious. It sets its own rules, welcomes surprises, is easy on its audience, and—unlike a show on or off Broadway—comes in a winner every time.

Every wife eventually learns that there are two kinds of menus, family and nonfamily. The former are as routine as brushing teeth. They *must* be routine or family life collapses. Just try changing the children's spaghetti-with-meat-sauce to green vermicelli with clams and artichoke hearts, and the unintended beneficiary will be either the psychological consultant for family problems or the attorney drawing up separation papers. But when intimate friends gather at midnight and the countless stars grow colder, when all the children lie slumbering under their blankets upstairs and hot coffee addicts begin nervously tapping their fingers, a whole new menu hand is open for play. The paprika chicken with yogurt that would send the youngsters into a hurricane of disapproval is now welcomed wolfishly by their elders. The good chafing dish of scrambled eggs with creamed smoked oysters no longer waits on appetite but can hardly keep up with it.

If you're so inclined, you can turn your midnight supper into the most extravagant of culinary productions. No law forbids you to make an aspic of crayfish that looks like the crown of an Eastern potentate. But pretentiousness in entertainment has become completely outdated in any private home and is in the worst possible taste at a midnight supper. The best modern cookery in the United States aims to be simple but imaginative. Amateur chefs are learning that tossing six herbs into a salad dressing doesn't make the dressing twice as good as one containing three herbs. As a matter of fact, the knack of using, but not adding too much of, any single herb—like tarragon, for instance—is the kind of finesse every intelligent homemaker aspires to. The soupçon rules the roost more effectively than ever.

Every cook works at her own pace. One woman can slice a loaf of French bread in a minute flat; another will take five minutes. One man can shuck clams faster than the eye can follow, while another moves with tortoise speed. But even allowing for these variations, this book of recipes is not an all-night cookbook. Most of the dishes actually involve very little cooking to be done at midnight. Last-minute reheating, last-minute sautéing, last-minute gratinéing are inevitable whenever hot foods are served. But these last-minute steps have been carefully planned so that the minutes don't snowball into hours.

Over the years, supper dishes have run the complete circle from cassoulets that take two days' preparation time to instant foods in dehydrated or frozen form that take two minutes. The trouble with most (though not all) of the fast factory foods is that they're like a romance that's grown stale. You may reconstitute them once and get away with it. But the second or third time around, too many of them are practiced bores. Most people don't resent a reasonable amount of time spent in cooking for their guests, provided the dish they offer is an artful achievement and so delicious that the night owls they've invited will chant its praises spontaneously. These days many a fine midnight dish is a combination of a prepared food in fresh form and an individual filling or sauce. If you need fresh cooked lobster or crab-meat, for example, you can buy them all ready for the saucepan or casserole without the unremitting and tedious labor that used to be necessary to prepare them from scratch. And Greek phyllo pastry, each leaf thinner than the sheerest summer voile, which involves hours of difficult and skilled preparation, is now available at Middle Eastern food stores in all parts of the United States. The phyllo leaves, stuffed with feta cheese and spinach—to take only one among countless possible combinations—are a delightful midsummery dream of a dish that can be baked at the last moment and served crispy hot and fragrant.

Nowadays many dishes for which one needs cooked chicken or turkey may be made from chicken or turkey roll or cooked breast of turkey. The best brands are refrigerator fresh with a moist succulence often far superior to the homemaker's leftover roast chicken with its flat, withered-on-the-carcass flavor.

An offering as pleasant as a patty of scallops can now be made with fresh patty shells from your neighborhood baker. They come to the table with the same fresh bloom of your own patty shells—preparation time about eighteen hours—and are usually more uniform in shape and size. How your patty of scallops finally comes to the midnight table, whether it's flavored with Madeira or white wine or both, whether it's combined with fresh mushrooms or water chestnuts, whether it's seasoned with shallots or scallions or chives, or spiced with paprika, curry, or dill-weed—these are only a few of the options possible.

How much of the supper shall be your own and how much procured from outside sources is a decision that is totally up to you. A housewife who has to prepare meals three times a day for young children can't, even if she wants to, plunge into a bottomless pit of work for a midnight supper. Nor can a busy career woman.

The intelligent alternative is to offer one or two dishes that are your own handiwork. Instead of the homemade platter of fussy canapés with their rosettes and their truffles cut into the shapes of stars and crescents, offer freshly roasted almonds and some luscious olives. Make the seafood and rice but skip the salad, buy a fresh dessert, and serve simple freshly brewed coffee. If you are in the mood for making a nesselrode turnover and this is your pride and joy, serve a platter of freshly sliced cold cuts from a gourmet meat counter without any elaborate burning of the midnight oil.

In a nutshell, the best advice is this: At a midnight supper you should unfold your hospitality with a single kitchen opus, or at the most two. No concert pianist in his right mind attempts to play all five Beethoven concerti in one evening.

In choosing any dish for a midnight supper, you will normally ask yourself, "Whom is it likely to please?" The Tom who likes Polish sausage may not agree with the Dick who favors panned clams or the Harry who always orders hot cakes. Broadly speaking, the best way to decide is to choose a dish that first of all pleases *you*. You don't master a dish in order to have its praises wasted on the desert air. You offer minute steaks with a sauce of deviled hollandaise not just because some of your party like minute steaks, but because this particular dish will cause your guests to react in a way that's pure butter to your ego. You can't tailor your menu to suit every stodgy little preference or cater to every food whim in the world. In an exceptional case, your common sense wouldn't allow you knowingly to offer scallops, for instance, to a person who you know has a violent reaction to this seafood. But generally, in choosing a dish for a midnight party, you want your guests' praise to be your own eventual joyride.

As far as possible, make the midnight supper suit the occasion. If you're planning an after-theater party, for instance, it's a sensible idea to counsel guests of whatever age to eat lightly beforehand both in order to stay awake during the show and to join subsequently in the substantial collation you've prepared. For an after-hockey, after-basketball, or similar party, let your guests know that hot cheese croûtes will be ready for them in a matter of minutes after they arrive. When a party of friends comes in late at night, weary after a long day on the turnpikes, a simple hot swiss cheese and potato soup will be the best possible comfort.

If you've invited friends simply for the pleasure of their company at midnight— a supper for supper's sake—the ideal dish is one that's substantial but not stolid. A hot German sauerbraten in its rich sweet-and-sour, ginger-flavored sauce would be Wotan-like even for veteran night owls. But a dish of sesame meat balls in a sweet-and-sour sauce would be heaven without heaviness. Many of the high-protein dishes of Chinese or Japanese origin, stir-fried in minutes, make magnificent intimate munching late at night.

Often the season itself decides the midnight dish. A tureen of crab chowder in the winter would do an about-face in the summer to a cold crab vichyssoise. Beginning with the "R" months in the fall, oysters in almost any style, from oyster stew to oyster shortcake, can always be depended upon to titillate the midnight crowd.

There are some people who fall into a shattered mental state the day they entertain invited guests—whether the entertainment be a brunch, a tea, a formal dinner, or a midnight supper. They beat their nerves as if they were smacking veal for scallopine until their transparent agony is almost too hard to bear. It's a common symptom of instability, and it can almost always be traced to simple lack of experience. In every case the answer to the problem is simple: rehearse. A woman who wouldn't think of wearing a dress that she had not tried on, studied, had altered and refitted with every nicety carefully judged, should follow the same routine when she's planning a midnight supper featuring a new dish still in the bib and jumper stage. Let you or your husband or both be judges in a dry run of the crepes a day or two before your party. Even if you're planning a dish as unpretentious as veal and onion hero sandwiches, it's a good idea to try the sandwiches beforehand for the sake of standing comfortably on your own feet at party time.

Sometimes, in some homes, the last-minute setting of the table, gathering chairs, plugging in and preheating utensils, searching for and washing platters, mixing and replenishing drinks, and other unmapped duties make both hostess and host look like a pair of overworked busboys. Most of these party duties have little to do with the actual cooking of a midnight supper. Telling you how to organize, simplify, and minimize them is the business of Chapter 1.

But no matter what plans you draft for your midnight supper, the ambience of your party should be as graciously informal as possible. The cordial buffet table, the self-serve platters or salad bowls—sometimes set up in the kitchen itself to make guests feel as freely at home as possible—are infinitely better than a stiff table at which guests are rigorously seated by sex and age with all the warmth of punch cards fed into a computer. The flame under your fondue pot should be lazily aglow. The melted cheese and kirsch should not bubble like a reactivated volcano about to overflow its rim, but should be quietly simmering as it waits for the midnight guests to come back again and again.

1

Before the Party

THE KEY to many a successful supper party is not how much money you spend but how you spend or share your time. And often it's not the total amount of time you lavish on preparations but how you apportion this precious commodity. Your goal —to have as much fun as your guests—will be that much closer if you can have an easy interval before they arrive, that is, have plenty of time to dress and enjoy a private joke or two with your spouse or cohost before the crowd arrives. Obviously this means that all possible advance work must be out of the way.

Long before the phrase women's lib was heard, many a wife and husband were sharing the details of party preparations. In getting ready for a party, whether a midnight supper or a Sunday morning brunch, the woman has usually assumed all the buying, cooking, and cleaning chores while the man confined himself to the duties of a bar host. But today countless men have culinary skills or specialties that amply qualify them for party cooking, and they eagerly take on the job. In the matter of shopping, too—which frequently takes an extravagant amount of time—men will often take the responsibility of ordering a particular pastry or going to a gourmet shop for specialty foods not available in the neighborhood.

As much shopping as possible should be done the day before the party. To make sure your list is thorough enough that you can complete the shopping in one or two trips, it's a good idea to review in detail both menu and recipes, and then put down in writing all the items needed, from paper goods to after-supper bonbons. Meats and poultry, as well as all staples like pasta, coffee, and mixes for drinks, should certainly be on hand the day before so that they are ready to be cooked or cooled on the morning of the party. Baked goods should be ordered in advance but picked up fresh the day they're to be served. Prepared seafood from the fish dealer, like cooked shrimp and lobster, should be ordered a day or two beforehand and picked up the day it's to be used. Obviously, if you're making a curry or soup that benefits by being held in the refrigerator a day or so before it's served, you'll need to plan your shopping accordingly.

All weekly household chores, if they're yours to do rather than a maid's, should be done the day before the party. No woman needs to be told that a last-minute tidying is always necessary, but she may need to be reminded—especially if she's a busy career woman or mother of young children—to check such amenities as guest towels and soap, extra coat hangers in the guest closet, cigarettes and ash-trays. If the fireplace is to be used, it should be glowing before guests arrive and there should be an ample supply of firewood readily at hand. Flowers are not the meat and drink of a late supper party, but a vase of fresh flowers is still a warm greeting, a beautiful detail of face-lifting in any room; guests notice and appreciate it.

The table for a midnight supper need not be set up to look like a bejeweled lady. Your tablecloth (or place mats) and napkins should be arranged on the table, and silverware and china may be in place, but you might want to avoid the stiffly regimented look of a formal dinner table and place the silver and china on the table just before suppertime. If you have a serving cart, the tableware and other accessories can be brought on along with the food in one trip. If you're using a chafing dish or hot tray, it should be in place all ready to be lit or plugged in.

Accessories like the serving cart or trays, serving spoons, dessert plates, and cups and saucers should be counted, stacked, and ready to go. The coffee maker should be ready to be plugged in and the teapot scalded and ready for brewing.

Your invitations must make it clear that you're serving a late supper and not just the routine coffee and cake. People may or may not want drinks at this hour. Certainly after an evening of ice-skating or skiing warm grog will be expected. After the theater, when guests gather to scorch or to praise the cast, script, and director, or after a tumultuous session at city hall or a school board meeting, leisurely highballs before supper are an interlude to remind guests that, though they may sound off to their hearts' content, they're still at a friendly social gathering and not in a pulpit. (Chapter 12 deals in detail with suitable drinks to serve at your party and how and when to serve them.)

Don't forget to fill your ice buckets beforehand and have plenty of ice in reserve, as well as a stack of coasters. Old-fashioned or on-the-rocks glasses are usually the bar glassware most in demand, but highball and cocktail glasses should also be available. The standard liquors and carbonated drinks should be within easy reach of your bar or liquor cabinet. If guests are apt to arrive from a political rally or sports event as thirsty as they are hungry, the serving of drinks can be facilitated by having ready a large quantity of a single drink, no questions asked. If it's one of the host's own specialties, so much the better. In the summer, pitchers of tall coolers fill the same role. Trays of the hot and cold canapés usually served with sundown drinks are the kind of fanfare that is completely out of place at an informal late-night supper. Freshly toasted salted nuts and other piquant diversions like corn chips or soy-flavored biscuits are more appropriate and not likely to dull appetites for the supper.

Most important of all, the supper itself should be the kind of food spelled out in this book, all ready to be popped in the oven or reheated over simmering water. If there is a last-minute job like boiling pasta or sautéing minute steaks, the ingredients should be portioned out and instantly ready for the fire, the necessary utensils or appliances all in place. If you've chosen a cold supper, even less last-minute preparation will be necessary. Whatever the dish you serve, it should be one that you have made at least once before; no matter how easy a dish may be in its conception, there will be even less waste motion if you've gone through the steps once. This doesn't mean that you should serve the same supper dish to the same friends over and over just because making it has become second nature to you. On the other hand, you should not use your friends as guinea pigs, particularly if you're undertaking something completely new.

Finally, for the post-supper cleanup, the easiest, but sometimes an appallingly expensive, solution is to hire a maid or bartender-butler. If the supper follows a concert or opera and the hosting couple as well as their guests are in formal evening wear, the idea of a maid makes sense. But for the informal drinking and eating of most supper parties, a hired servant seems to cut a pretentious figure, and husband and wife will probably prefer to handle the chores themselves, working out an acceptable routine in advance for doing so.

Before guests arrive it's always helpful if the kitchen dishwasher is emptied ready to receive a new load. Before and during supper, such details as removing glasses and replacing ashtrays may be handled by either husband or wife. The job of clearing the supper table quickly and unobtrusively while the guests are still seated can easily be worked out beforehand. Either husband or wife should always remain with the guests while the other assumes this chore. Sometimes, while the host is in the kitchen for a few moments waiting for the supper food or coffee, he or she can partially load the dishwasher with used glasses or dishes. The chores are really minimal at a midnight collation, and when handled without fuss, the final tidying seems insignificant in the pleasant afterglow of a happy supper party.

Recipes for Eight

All recipes in this book are planned for a party of eight.

Portions, servings—call them what you will—are not allotted by heaven's will or by fate but simply by the author of a recipe. A nine-inch pie may satisfy six or eight or at times twelve appetites; one man's platter of pasta for dinner may be portions for three or four at midnight. Fortunately, the hostess planning a supper usually knows something of her guests' capacities and habits at the table, and she can—in fact, she must—be sufficiently flexible to hold the scales even and prepare the amount of food she thinks is fitting. If your crowd always demands second helpings, you will know this beforehand and should govern your buying and preparation accordingly. If you are the kind of person who consistently prepares too much, there's always the consolation that if the dish is exquisitely delicious on the evening of your supper, it will be more than a pleasant memory the next day, when the scene of the previous night's party is happily retraced.

❡ This paragraph in each recipe indicates the preparations to be made at the last moment.

NOTE: Some of the recipes that follow call for chopping, dicing, or shredding particular ingredients. Before you sharpen your knife, be sure to read the instructions which give the exact method of preparation.

2
〰

Soups

ANYONE who remembers the lively aroma of the bubbling hot onion soup and parmesan cheese served for generations in Les Halles, the old produce market in Paris, will appreciate how much better any soup can be when offered very late at night. In Paris it was usually served at dawn after a night's carousal. Soups at midnight are for people who love oyster bars, for those who will happily endure the coldest ski slopes or the wintry blasts at a football bowl game knowing that a tureen of hot oyster stew is waiting to comfort them near a toasty fireplace. On a summer night on a cool terrace a cold soup of the vichyssoise family will be equally comforting. Soups of this genre do not, of course, include decorous thin consommés or other clear broths served in a tiny *tasse*.

No matter what time of the day or night they're served, soups are always better for having been made in advance and hibernating a day, or at least a half day, in the refrigerator. Flavors of stock, vegetables, and seafoods join in a mellow camaraderie that's missing if the soup is made just before serving. This doesn't mean that endless slow cooking will produce the same gentle flavors as one finds in a day-old soup. As a matter of fact, when making the thick seafood soups—misnamed stews—it's extremely important to avoid initial overcooking or the seafood will turn to rubber. Vegetables for soups, either diced or julienne, should be cut with almost machinelike uniformity not only for uniform cooking but for simple eye appeal. Although fat on the surface of soups made from meat or poultry is normally skimmed off, seafood stews are expected to have a distinct golden sheen of butter on top.

Soup may be reheated over a direct flame, but if it contains milk or cream, which scorches easily, you must tend the soup pot frequently and bring it up only to the boiling point. If the soup contains seafood, it should be served as soon as it is hot. Using a double boiler for reheating requires less attention, and if yours isn't large enough to hold soup for eight people, you can improvise a steam table by placing a large pot with the soup in a deep baking pan; add one or two inches of hot water to the pan, depending on the pan's depth, and heat it over one or two flames. Replace water as necessary, since it may boil down rather quickly, and keep the water simmering rather than boiling.

The bowls for hot soup should be warmed beforehand; place them in a slow oven for a few minutes. Bowls for cold soup should be prechilled; place them in the freezer for a few minutes. The most gracious way of serving soup is from a tureen. If your tureen isn't large enough, initial portions may be served from the kitchen in bowls and refills offered from the tureen at the table.

Seafood stews or soups should be accompanied by the traditional oyster, trenton, or pilot crackers, or all three. Open fresh packages of crackers for your soup party; if they need freshening, place them in a shallow pan in a slow oven until heated through; let them cool before serving. When onion soup of one variety or another is offered, small crisp hard rolls, crisp French bread, and sourdough French bread are all wonderful grist for the midnight soup meal.

Alsatian Onion Soup with Cream

1 quart Spanish onions, thinly sliced	1 cup heavy cream
½ cup finely minced shallots or scallions, white part	Salt
	White pepper
1 tablespoon finely minced garlic	32 slices narrow French bread ¼
6 tablespoons butter	inch thick, toasted under broiler
3 quarts chicken broth, fresh or canned	Parmesan cheese, freshly grated
	Paprika

Peel onions and cut in half through stem end. Cut crosswise into thinnest possible slices. To peel shallots place flat side of heavy French knife on one or two shallots on cutting board. Hit knife with fist to partly smash shallots. Peel will then come off easily before mincing. Garlic may be handled in same manner. If scallions are used, cut them crosswise into very thin slices. Melt butter in soup pot. Add onions, shallots or scallions, and garlic. Sauté over low flame, stirring almost constantly, until onions are light yellow. Do not let them brown. Add chicken broth. Bring to a boil, reduce flame, and simmer 20 minutes. Add cream, bring up to the boiling point, and remove from flame. Add salt if necessary. Season quite generously with pepper. Chill.

❧ Preheat oven at 450 degrees. Bring soup up to a boil. Pour into eight 12-ounce individual French marmites, dividing onions equally among marmites. Float 4 slices toast on top of soup in each pot. A couple of slices will be absorbed by soup, the others will stick up somewhat. Sprinkle generously with cheese. Sprinkle lightly with paprika. Place marmites in a large roasting pan, pour 1 inch hot water into pan, and bake 20 to 30 minutes or until cheese topping is well browned. Remove pan carefully with heavy potholders or move oven shelf forward and lift marmites out one at a time. Warn guests that marmites and soup are mad hot. Soup may be eaten directly from marmites or ladled by each guest into a soup plate. Pass additional parmesan cheese at table.

Onion and Fresh Tomato Soup

1 quart and 1 pint Spanish onions, thinly sliced
1½ cups fresh tomatoes peeled and cut in thin strips
Butter
2 tablespoons salad oil
2 teaspoons garlic minced extremely fine
2 quarts and 1 cup chicken broth, fresh or canned
1 teaspoon crushed whole pepper
1 teaspoon worcestershire sauce
32 slices narrow French bread, ¼ inch thick
Parmesan cheese, freshly grated
Oregano

To prepare onions, peel and cut in half through stem end. Cut crosswise into thinnest possible slices. To prepare tomatoes, dip in boiling water for 20 seconds. Remove skin and stem end. Cut into sixths and squeeze to remove seeds. Cut into thinnest possible lengthwise strips to make 1½ cups. In soup pot heat 2 tablespoons butter with salad oil until butter melts. Add onions, garlic, and tomatoes. Sauté, stirring frequently, until onions are limp and yellow. Add broth, pepper, and worcestershire sauce. Bring to a boil. Lower flame, skim soup, and simmer 20 minutes. Chill. Spread bread generously on one side with butter. Sprinkle buttered side generously with parmesan cheese and lightly with oregano. Place bread slices on cookie sheets or shallow baking pans and cover with clear plastic wrap.

❡ Preheat oven at 375 degrees. Bake cheese croutons 15 to 20 minutes or until brown around edges. Reheat soup up to the boiling point. Pass croutons and parmesan cheese separately at table.

Onion Soup with Ditalini, Provolone Croutons

1 quart Spanish onions, thinly sliced
6 tablespoons butter
2 teaspoons garlic minced extremely fine
3 quarts chicken or beef broth, fresh or canned
1 cup ditalini (very small tubular macaroni)
Salt
Pepper
Cayenne pepper
2 teaspoons worcestershire sauce
32 slices narrow French bread, ¼ inch thick
½ pound provolone cheese, unsliced
Paprika
1 tablespoon parsley very finely minced
Parmesan cheese, freshly grated

Peel onions and cut in half through stem end. Cut crosswise into thinnest possible slices. Melt butter in a soup pot over a low flame. Add onions and garlic. Sauté, stirring frequently, until onions are a light yellow. Add chicken broth. Bring to a boil. Reduce flame and simmer 20 minutes. In another pot bring to a rapid boil 2 quarts of water to which 1 tablespoon salt has been added. Stir in ditalini. Cook 12 to 15 minutes or until ditalini are tender. Drain. Place drained ditalini, covered with cold water, in container. Chill. Season soup with salt and pepper to taste, a dash of cayenne, and worcestershire sauce. Chill. Preheat broiler. Place bread on cookie sheet or shallow baking pan and toast until light brown on both sides. Shred provolone cheese by forcing it through large holes of metal grater and sprinkle on bread. Sprinkle lightly with paprika. Chill.

❢ Preheat oven at 350 degrees. Bake cheese croutons 10 minutes or until cheese is melted. Drain ditalini well, add to soup, and reheat up to boiling point. Add parsley. Stir soup well before serving. Pass croutons and parmesan cheese at table.

Swiss Cheese and Potato Soup

1 pound swiss cheese, shredded
⅓ cup butter
1 cup finely diced onions
½ cup thinly sliced leeks, white part only
1 teaspoon very finely minced garlic
1 teaspoon dried summer savory
3 cups finely diced potatoes
1 quart chicken broth, fresh or canned
3 cups milk
1 cup light cream
¼ cup parmesan cheese, freshly grated
Salt
Pepper
1 package prepared or fresh bread croutons, diced and oven toasted

Shred swiss cheese by forcing it through large holes of metal grater and set aside. Melt butter in large soup pot. Add onions, leeks, garlic, and summer savory. Sauté until onions are limp. Add potatoes and chicken broth. Bring to a boil, reduce flame, and simmer until potatoes are tender. Add milk and cream and bring up to the boiling point but do not boil. Stir in parmesan cheese. Add salt and pepper to taste. Chill.

❡ Reheat over simmering water. Reheat bread croutons in preheated oven at 350 degrees for 5 minutes. When soup is hot enough to serve, take off the fire, and stir in swiss cheese. Correct seasoning if necessary. Pass croutons separately at table.

Italian Cheese Soup

½ pound provolone cheese, shredded
½ pound fontina cheese, shredded
4 tablespoons butter
¼ pound thinly sliced prosciutto ham or Canadian bacon, very finely chopped
1 cup finely diced onions
1 teaspoon very finely minced garlic
¾ cup finely diced celery
6 cups chicken broth
6 cups cold milk
¾ cup instant dissolving flour
1 cup light cream
Salt
Pepper
3 cups white bread cubed, ½ inch thick
¼ cup olive oil
2 tablespoons grated parmesan cheese

Shred provolone and fontina cheeses by forcing them through large holes of metal grater and set aside. Melt butter over low flame. Add prosciutto or Canadian bacon, onions, garlic, and celery. Sauté only until onions are soft, not brown. Add chicken broth. Bring to a boil. Reduce flame and simmer slowly. In a mixing bowl, dissolve flour in milk, beating with wire whip or rotary beater. Add milk and cream to soup. Bring to a boil. Reduce flame and simmer 10 minutes. Add shredded cheese. Continue to simmer, stirring constantly, until cheese is completely melted. Remove from fire. Add salt and pepper to taste. Chill. Preheat oven at 350 degrees. In a large bowl toss bread cubes with oil and parmesan cheese. Place bread on a cookie sheet and bake, stirring occasionally, until croutons are browned, about 15 to 20 minutes.

❡ Reheat soup in double boiler. Pass croutons at table.

Oyster Stew with Mushrooms and Shallots

6 dozen medium-size oysters, shucked
⅓ cup finely minced shallots or scallions, white part
½ pound fresh mushrooms
½ pound butter
1 tablespoon worcestershire sauce
¼ teaspoon Tabasco sauce
Salt
Celery salt
White pepper
Paprika
2 quarts milk
1 pint light cream

Remove mushroom caps from stems. If caps are large, cut in half. Cut caps and stems in very thin slices. Melt ¼ pound butter in large saucepan. Sauté mushrooms and shallots until mushrooms are tender. Add oysters and sauté only until oysters curl around edges. Add worcestershire sauce and Tabasco. Season with salt, celery salt, white pepper, and paprika. Chill.

❡ Reheat oyster mixture. In a separate saucepan bring milk and cream up to a boil. Cut remaining butter into 8 tablespoons. Combine oysters and milk mixture. Correct seasoning if necessary. Place 9 oysters in each individual serving bowl and fill with milk mixture. Add a tablespoon butter to each bowl. Sprinkle generously with paprika. Serve with an assortment of oyster crackers, trenton crackers, and pilot crackers.

Oyster Stew Nelson

6 dozen medium-size oysters, shucked
6 large stalks celery, including tops, sliced
1 large Spanish onion, sliced
2 carrots, sliced
12 sprigs parsley
6 sprigs dill
4 quarts water
2 sticks butter, ¼ pound each
Salt
Celery salt
Dill salt
Paprika
Pepper
1 pint milk
1 pint heavy cream
2 teaspoons worcestershire sauce

Boil celery, onion, carrots, parsley, and dill in 4 quarts water to which 2 teaspoons salt have been added until 4 quarts are reduced to approximately 1½ quarts. Strain stock and discard vegetables. Chill stock. Melt ¼ pound butter in large saucepan. Add oysters. Season generously with salt, celery salt, dill salt, paprika, and pepper. Sauté only until oysters begin to curl around edges. Chill.

❡ Reheat oysters over a low flame only until oysters are warmed. In a separate saucepan heat stock, milk, and cream up to the boiling point. Add worcestershire sauce. Correct seasoning if necessary. Divide remaining ¼ pound butter into 8 tablespoons. Place 9 oysters in each individual soup bowl. Fill bowl with milk. Add a tablespoon butter to each bowl. Sprinkle generously with paprika. Serve with an assortment of oyster crackers, trenton crackers, and pilot crackers.

Curried Oyster, Shrimp, and Apple Stew

3 dozen large-size oysters, drained and shucked
1 pound shelled shrimp, freshly cooked (2 pounds raw shrimp in shell)
4 large delicious apples
Flour
Salad oil
12 tablespoons butter (1½ sticks)
¾ cup finely minced onions
1½ teaspoons curry powder
Salt
Celery salt
White pepper
2 cups clam juice, bottled or fresh
1 quart and 1 pint milk
1 cup heavy cream

Peel and core apples. Apples may be dipped in fruit juice to prevent discoloration. Cut apples into sixths through stem end. Cut each sixth crosswise into 3 parts. Dip apples in flour and shake off excess flour. Heat two tablespoons oil in large frying pan and sauté apple pieces until tender and light brown. Turn frequently while sautéing, adding more oil if necessary. Remove apples from pan and set aside. In a large saucepan melt 6 tablespoons butter over a low flame. Add onions and sauté only until onions are tender, not brown. Stir in curry powder. Add oysters and shrimp. Season generously with salt, celery salt, and white pepper. Sauté until oysters begin to curl around edges. Add clam juice and bring up to boiling point. Add apples. Chill.

❮ Reheat stew over low flame. Add balance of butter. In a separate pot heat milk and cream up to the boiling point. Add milk and cream to stew. Correct seasoning if necessary. Serve with an assortment of oyster crackers, trenton crackers, and pilot crackers.

Cream Shrimp Stew with Catsup

2 pounds shrimp, freshly cooked, peeled, and deveined
  (4 pounds raw shrimp in shell)
¼ pound butter
¼ cup finely minced shallots or scallions, white part
2 tablespoons very finely minced fresh parsley
½ teaspoon dried tarragon
½ teaspoon dried chervil
¼ teaspoon ground fennel
1 cup tomato catsup
1 quart milk
1 quart light cream
Salt
Pepper
Celery salt
4 tablespoons butter
Paprika

Melt ¼ pound butter in large soup pot. Add shallots or scallions, parsley, tarragon, chervil, ground fennel, catsup, and shrimp. Mix well. Add milk and cream. Very slowly bring up to a boil, but do not boil. Add salt, pepper, and celery salt to taste. Chill.

❡ Reheat stew over very low flame or over simmering water. Break up 4 tablespoons butter and stir into stew until it melts. Sprinkle with paprika. Serve with an assortment of oyster crackers, trenton crackers, and pilot crackers.

Crab Meat Chowder, Shrimp Dumplings

1 pound fresh shrimp
2 egg whites, slightly beaten
1 cup light cream
1 small onion, grated
Salt
Celery salt
White pepper
1 large onion, sliced
2 pieces celery, sliced

¼ cup butter
1½ cups diced onions
½ cup diced celery
1 teaspoon very finely minced garlic
¼ cup flour
2 cups diced potatoes
1 pound fresh deluxe crab lump or 2 cans
    (7¾ ounces each) fancy crab meat
1 quart milk

Peel and devein shrimp, saving shells. Put shrimp through meat grinder twice using fine blade. Place in freezer about 20 minutes to chill. Turn shrimp into electric mixer. At low speed, very slowly, about a teaspoon at a time, add egg whites. At same speed, add ½ cup of the cream and grated onion. Season with ¼ teaspoon salt, ¼ teaspoon celery salt, and dash of white pepper. Bring 1½ inches water to a boil in a wide pot or dutch oven. Add ground shrimp mixture, about a teaspoon at a time, to boiling water to make dumplings. Do not crowd pot. Boil, covered, about 5 minutes. Remove dumplings with slotted spoon or skimmer. Chill dumplings. Add enough water to pot to make 2 quarts. Add shrimp shells, 1 teaspoon salt, sliced onion, and sliced celery. Boil until 2 quarts are reduced to 1 quart liquid. Strain. Sauté diced onions, diced celery, and garlic in butter until onions are tender but not brown. Stir in flour, blending well. Add shrimp stock and potatoes. Simmer until potatoes are tender. Examine crab meat carefully, removing any pieces of shell or cartilage. Add crab meat to pot. Add milk, remaining ½ cup cream, and dumplings. Slowly bring up to a boil. Correct seasoning. Chill.

❡ Reheat chowder over simmering water or over low flame. Serve with oyster crackers or trenton crackers.

Cold Cream of Cucumber Soup

3 cups cucumber, rind left on, cut into ½ inch cubes
¼ cup butter
1 medium-size clove garlic, finely minced
2 medium-size onions, thinly sliced
1 large leek, white part only, sliced
¼ teaspoon dried chervil or 1 teaspoon fresh chervil
1 quart chicken broth, fresh or canned

2 cups potatoes peeled and thinly sliced
2 cups milk
½ cup light cream
Salt
White pepper
2 scallions
3 red radishes
1½ cups sour cream

This soup should be made the day before it's served, or no later than the morning of the day it's to be served. Melt butter in a soup pot. Don't let butter brown. Add garlic, onions, leek, and chervil. Sauté only until onion turns yellow; don't allow to brown. Add chicken broth and potatoes. Simmer until potatoes are tender. Add milk and cream. Bring up to a boil, but do not boil. Cool slightly. Pour soup together with raw cucumbers into blender. Don't fill blender more than half full at a time. Blend until smooth. Add salt and pepper to taste. Chill in refrigerator. Cut scallions, including white and solid part of green, into thinnest possible crosswise slices. Force radishes through large holes of metal grater. Mix scallions and radishes with sour cream. Chill. Place soup cups or bowls in refrigerator to chill until serving time.

❡ Stir soup well. Thin with milk if it seems too thick. Pour into cups or bowls. Add a dollop of sour cream mixture on top or pass at table.

Cold Curried Crab Vichyssoise

1 pound fresh deluxe crab lump or 2 cans (7¾ ounces each) fancy crab meat
⅓ cup butter
1½ cups sliced onions
1 cup sliced leeks, white part only
1 teaspoon very finely minced garlic
3 cups sliced potatoes
4 cups chicken broth, fresh or canned
2 cups milk
1 cup light cream
1 tablespoon curry powder
Salt
Pepper
2 tablespoons very finely minced fresh chives

Examine crab meat carefully and remove any pieces of shell or cartilage. Melt butter in soup pot. Add onions, leeks, and garlic. Sauté only until onions are yellow; do not brown. Add potatoes and chicken broth. Bring to a boil. Reduce flame and simmer until potatoes are very soft. Let mixture cool slightly. Add half the crab meat to mixture. Turn mixture into blender to puree, doing job in two or three batches if necessary. Blend until smooth. Return mixture to soup pot. Add milk and cream. Bring up to the boiling point but do not boil. Stir curry powder with 2 tablespoons cold water. Add to pot. Add salt and pepper to taste. Add balance of crab meat. Chill.

❡ Before serving, correct seasoning and thin soup with additional cold milk if necessary. Sprinkle on chives just before serving.

Cold Sorrel Vichyssoise

¾ pound sorrel*
4 tablespoons butter
2 cups onions diced medium fine
1 teaspoon very finely minced garlic
3 cups potatoes diced medium fine
6 cups chicken broth
2 cups milk
1 cup heavy cream
2 tablespoons lemon juice
Salt
Pepper
1½ cups sour cream
2 tablespoons very finely minced chives

Wash sorrel well, discarding any leaves that are spoiled. Melt butter in a soup pot. Add onions and garlic. Sauté until onions are soft but not browned. Add sorrel, potatoes, and chicken broth and simmer ½ hour. Let soup cool slightly. Pour into blender in small batches and blend smooth. In another pan bring milk and cream up to the boiling point. Add to soup. Pour soup through a large wire strainer. Remove and discard any tough fiber or unblended solid pieces. Add lemon juice and salt and pepper to taste. Chill thoroughly. Mix sour cream and chives.

❡ If soup seems too thick at serving time, thin it with additional milk. Pass sour cream separately at table.

* Obtainable in specialty vegetable stores; known as sour grass.

3

~

Hot Sandwiches

SANDWICHES FOR A long time were handicapped by two traditions but have successfully lived them both down. The first one, traditionally promulgated by the eighteenth-century inventor of the snack, the Earl of Sandwich, led people to believe that a sandwich was something to be eaten in a room filled with dense smoke and cardplayers. It was the kind of food you didn't look at but simply wolfed down while your eyes were more profitably riveted on your hand of poker, pinochle, or bridge. The second tradition was that of the dainty mousse-filled tea sandwich designed to kill the appetite temporarily and as inconspicuously as possible, not to make it happy. Neither of these traditions stood much of a chance when people began discovering the joys of thick corned beef or pastrami or tongue sandwiches, and combinations of these meats, served warm and thinly sliced on sour rye bread. Hot sandwiches for midnight gatherings range from the flat Mideastern pita filled like a thick pocket to husky heroes eaten in hand to French toasted sandwiches that are always eaten with knife and fork but in as pleasantly informal a manner as possible.

Sandwiches assembled beforehand and stored in the refrigerator should always be carefully covered with tight-fitting clear plastic wrap to prevent bread and other ingredients from drying. The usual white sandwich bread should be a day old for best handling, while pitas, rolls, and hero buns should be bakery fresh. Butter or margarine for sandwiches should be unsalted if possible. To soften butter, let it stand at room temperature until it can be spread easily; in warm weather or in a very warm kitchen, however, when butter may melt, it's best to let it stand briefly at room temperature and then work it with a knife or spatula until it's plastic enough to be spread smoothly without tearing the bread.

Cold beer or ale and an attractive compartmented tray or lazy susan with cold relishes and pickles belong on the sandwich party table.

Deviled Ham and Port Salut Sandwiches

8 kaiser rolls or club rolls
Soft butter or margarine
1 pound Virginia style baked ham, sliced very thin
8 ounce can water chestnuts, drained
Catsup
2 tablespoons bottled sauce diable
1 tablespoon prepared mustard
12 ounces port salut cheese, thinly sliced

Cut rolls in half horizontally. Scrape out several tablespoons of soft centers of both halves, and discard. Spread rolls to edge with butter. Cut ham into very small dice, no more than $\frac{1}{16}$ inch square, or put through meat grinder using coarse blade. Cut or grind the water chestnuts in the same manner. Mix ham, water chestnuts, $\frac{1}{2}$ cup catsup, sauce diable, and mustard. Spoon ham mixture onto all roll halves. Place cheese on top, trimming slices if necessary to fit within margin of rolls. Spread cheese lightly with catsup. Chill.

❡ Preheat oven at 350 degrees. Bake 10 to 12 minutes. Serve as hot open sandwiches.

Shrimp, Provolone, and Pimiento Sandwiches

8 kaiser rolls or club rolls
Soft butter or margarine
1 pound (cooked weight) shrimp, boiled, shelled, and deveined
   (2 pounds raw shrimp)
4 jars (2 ounces each) pimiento strips, drained
¼ cup capers in vinegar, drained
2 cups thick cream sauce (recipe follows at end of chapter, p. 50)
1 medium-size onion, grated
2 tablespoons lemon juice
Salt
Pepper
12 ounces provolone cheese, sliced thin

Cut rolls in half horizontally. Scrape out several tablespoons of soft centers of both halves. Spread rolls to edge with butter. Cut shrimp into very small dice, no more than $1/16$ inch thick, or put through meat grinder using coarse blade. Mix shrimp with pimiento, capers, cream sauce, onion, and lemon juice. Add salt and pepper to taste. Spoon shrimp mixture onto all roll halves. Cut provolone cheese into strips ½ inch wide. Place strips, not touching each other, on top of shrimp mixture. Chill.

❡ Preheat oven at 350 degrees. Bake 10 to 12 minutes. Serve as hot open sandwiches.

Curried Shrimp, Bacon, and Tomato Sandwiches

8 kaiser rolls or club rolls
Soft butter or margarine
24 slices bacon
2 pounds ripe fresh tomatoes
1 pound (cooked weight) shrimp, boiled, shelled, and deveined
  (2 pounds raw shrimp)
8 ounce can water chestnuts, drained
1 cup mayonnaise
1 tablespoon curry powder
1 tablespoon lemon juice
Salt
Pepper

Cut rolls in half horizontally. Scrape out several tablespoons of soft centers of both halves, and discard. Spread rolls to edge with butter. Panfry the bacon until almost done. Drain bacon and cut slices in half crosswise. Cut tomatoes into thin slices. Cut shrimp into very small dice, no more than $1/16$ inch thick, or put through grinder using coarse blade. Cut or grind water chestnuts in the same manner. Mix shrimp, water chestnuts, mayonnaise, curry powder, and lemon juice. Add salt and pepper to taste. Spoon shrimp mixture onto all roll halves. Place tomato slices on top, fitting slices within margin of rolls. Sprinkle with salt. Place 3 pieces of bacon on each roll half. Chill.

❡ Preheat oven at 350 degrees. Bake 10 to 12 minutes. Serve as hot open sandwiches.

Lamb Ball and Pita Sandwiches

12 to 16 pitas (flat Mideast type bread)
2 pounds ground lamb
2 slices stale white bread
1 medium-size onion, grated
2 teaspoons very finely minced parsley
½ teaspoon oregano
½ teaspoon crumbled dried mint leaves
4 teaspoons lemon juice
2 teaspoons salt
¼ teaspoon ground black pepper
2 eggs, beaten
½ cup sweet peppers in vinegar, drained and very finely minced
Flour
Salad oil

NOTE: Guests assemble this sandwich at table, splitting pitas and filling them like pockets.

Soak 2 slices stale bread in cold water. Squeeze gently to remove excess water. Combine all ingredients except pitas, flour, and oil. Mix very well. Shape into small balls no larger than 1 inch in diameter. Dip lamb balls in flour and reshape if necessary by rolling lightly between palms of hands. Heat ¼ inch oil in electric skillet preheated at 370 degrees. Fry lamb balls till light brown, turning to brown evenly. Chill.

❧ Preheat oven at 350 degrees. Warm pitas 5 minutes. Cut in half crosswise. Place lamb balls in a very shallow pan and reheat about 20 minutes. Pass CUCUMBERS IN YOGURT and GREEK TOMATO SALAD (recipes follow), which should be made several hours ahead.

Cucumbers in Yogurt

4 cups sliced cucumbers
1 cup yogurt
1 tablespoon very finely minced fresh chives
Salt
Pepper

Peel cucumbers, cut in half lengthwise, and scrape out seeds with spoon. Cut crosswise into very thin slices. Combine yogurt with cucumbers and chives. Add salt and pepper to taste. Chill.

Greek Tomato Salad

1 pound fresh tomatoes
2 cups onions, thinly sliced
2 large bay leaves, chopped fine
½ cup olive oil
¼ cup fresh lemon juice
Salt
Pepper
Sugar

Lower tomatoes into boiling water for 20 seconds. Hold briefly under cold running water. Remove skins and stem from tomatoes. Cut tomatoes into quarters and press to remove seeds. Cut tomatoes into very thin slices. Break onion slices into strips. Heat oil and bay leaves a few minutes in a wide saucepan over a moderate flame. Add onions and tomatoes. Sauté, stirring constantly, until onions are limp but not browned. Turn contents of pan into mixing bowl. Stir in lemon juice, salt and pepper to taste, and a dash of sugar. Chill.

Pork Ball and Pita Sandwiches

12 to 16 pitas (flat Mideast type bread)
2 pounds ground pork shoulder or loin
2 slices stale white bread
1 teaspoon very finely minced garlic
2 eggs
2 teaspoons salt
1/4 teaspoon freshly ground black pepper
1/2 teaspoon ground sage
1/2 teaspoon ground cumin
Flour
Salad oil

NOTE: Guests assemble this sandwich at table, splitting pitas and filling them like pockets.

Soak 2 slices stale bread in cold water. Squeeze gently to remove excess water. Combine all ingredients except pitas, flour and oil. Mix very well. Shape into small balls no larger than 1 inch in diameter. Dip pork balls in flour and reshape if necessary by rolling lightly between palms of hands. Heat 1/4 inch oil in electric skillet preheated at 370 degrees. Fry pork balls till well browned, turning to brown evenly. Chill.

❦ Preheat oven at 350 degrees. Warm pitas 5 minutes. Cut in half crosswise. Place pork balls in a very shallow pan and reheat about 20 minutes. Pass CUCUMBERS IN YOGURT and GREEK TOMATO SALAD (see facing page), which should be made several hours ahead.

Marinated Lamb and Pita Sandwiches

12 to 16 pitas (flat Mideast type bread)
Half leg of lamb (3 to 3½ pounds) boned
½ cup salad oil
1½ teaspoons ground cumin
1½ teaspoons salt

½ teaspoon pepper
½ teaspoon ground cinnamon
1 large onion, sliced
Salad oil

NOTE: Guests assemble this sandwich at table, splitting pitas and filling them like pockets.

Remove all gristle, fat, and outer skin from lamb. With a very sharp knife cut lamb into slices no more than ⅛ inch thick and about 1 to 1½ inches square. Uniformly thick slices are important for proper cooking. Mix lamb with ½ cup salad oil, cumin, salt, pepper, and cinnamon. Toss well. Add onion slices to mixture. Cover. Refrigerate 5 to 6 hours or overnight.

❡ Preheat oven at 350 degrees. Warm pitas 5 minutes. Cut in half crosswise. Remove onion slices from lamb. Preheat a large electric skillet, or if possible 2 skillets, at 400 degrees. Brush skillet lightly with salad oil. Sauté lamb, turning frequently, until medium brown. Serve at once with pitas. Pass RADISH MINT RELISH (recipe follows), which may be made several hours ahead.

Radish Mint Relish

1 bunch red radishes, slice very thin
1 cup sour cream
1 tablespoon finely minced
　　fresh chives

24 large fresh mint leaves,
　　finely minced
Salt
Pepper

Mix radishes, sour cream, chives, and mint. Add salt and pepper to taste. Chill.

Chicken and Veal Caraway Cheeseburgers

8 hamburger buns, split
1½ pounds (trimmed weight) chicken breasts, boneless and skinless
1 pound veal, cut as for scaloppine
3 cups stale bread cut in ½ inch cubes
1 medium-size onion, sliced
2½ teaspoons salt
¼ teaspoon pepper
⅛ teaspoon freshly grated nutmeg
Salad oil
Butter
12 ounces caraway cheese, sliced

Cut away gristle in center of each chicken breast. Cut chicken and veal into large dice. Soak bread in cold water. Squeeze gently to eliminate excess water. Put chicken, veal, bread, and onion through meat grinder twice, using fine blade. Add salt, pepper, and nutmeg to meat mixture. Avoid overhandling meat mixture to keep patties light. Form meat into 16 patties of about ⅓ cup each. Score patties by making crisscross diagonal lines lightly with a knife on top and bottom. Lightly grease a large skillet with oil and preheat over a moderate flame. Sauté patties until medium brown on both sides. Toast cut side of buns lightly under a broiler. Spread buns with butter. Place a patty on each bun half. Spread patties generously with butter. Cut cheese so that a piece will cover each patty and place a slice of cheese on each patty. Place on a shallow baking pan or cookie sheet. Chill.

❏ Preheat oven at 375 degrees. Bake cheeseburgers 10 to 12 minutes.

Chicken Cutlet and Pepper Salad Sandwiches

8 large club rolls
1½ pounds (trimmed weight) chicken breasts, boneless and skinless
Salad oil
Salt
Pepper
Freshly grated nutmeg
Bread crumbs
3 eggs, beaten
⅓ cup milk
Soft butter or margarine
16 ounce jar pepper salad in oil
½ pound port salut cheese, thinly sliced
1 cup tomato sauce
¼ cup heavy sweet cream

Cut away any cartilage from center of chicken breasts. Remove long filet from underside of chicken. Set aside. Cut chicken breasts lengthwise in half. Pound all chicken with a meat mallet or side of cleaver until chicken is thin (as for veal scaloppine) but not torn. Cut chicken into pieces about 2 inches square. Brush lightly with oil. Sprinkle with salt, pepper, and nutmeg. Dip in bread crumbs. Beat eggs with milk. Dip chicken in eggs and again in bread crumbs, patting crumbs to make coating stick. Heat ¼ inch oil in large skillet. Sauté chicken until medium brown, wiping pan clean and replacing oil when necessary. Cut rolls in half lengthwise. Spread with butter. Place desired amount of pepper salad on rolls. Place chicken over pepper salad on rolls, arranging pieces so that portions are equal. Place a slice of cheese about 1 inch wide in center of sandwich. Chill. Combine tomato sauce and cream. Chill.

❡ Preheat oven at 375 degrees. Spoon tomato sauce on cheese. Bake 10 to 12 minutes.

Curried Sole and Bacon Open Sandwiches

16 slices white sandwich bread
Soft butter or margarine
1½ pounds fresh gray sole filets
16 slices bacon
Salt
Celery salt
Pepper
2 cups mayonnaise
2 tablespoons curry powder
2 teaspoons very finely minced fresh chives
2 tablespoons heavy cream
Bread crumbs
3 eggs beaten with ¼ cup water
Salad oil

Toast bread on one side only under broiler flame. Spread untoasted side with butter. Place bread, toasted side down, on greased shallow pans or cookie sheets. Cut sole lengthwise down center. Cut sole crosswise so that pieces of fish are no longer than bread slices. Wash and dry fish with paper toweling. Sprinkle with salt, celery salt, and pepper. Mix mayonnaise and curry powder. Set aside one cup mayonnaise mixture. Add to reserved mayonnaise the chives and heavy cream to be served as a dip later. Cover and chill. Spread balance of mayonnaise mixture on filets. Dip filets in bread crumbs. Dip in eggs. Again dip in crumbs, patting crumbs into fish so that coating is firm. Heat ¼ inch salad oil in electric skillet preheated at 370 degree. Fry sole until light brown. Wipe skillet clean and replace oil when necessary to avoid burnt crumbs on skillet bottom. Arrange fish on toast. Panfry the bacon until almost done. Arrange bacon slices on sole. Chill.

❡ Preheat oven at 375 degrees. Bake sandwiches 10 to 12 minutes. Pass curry dip at table.

Veal and Onion Hero Sandwiches

8 hero sandwich buns
Soft butter or margarine
2 pounds veal, cut as for scaloppine
Milk
1 large Spanish onion, about 1 pound
Salt
Pepper

Oregano
2 eggs
Salad oil
Bread crumbs
2 tablespoons red wine vinegar
2 anchovy filets, finely chopped
4 medium-size ripe tomatoes

Pound veal with meat mallet (or have butcher do it for you) until veal is as thin as possible but not torn. Soak veal in milk 1 hour. Place unpeeled onion in shallow pan in oven preheated at 275 degrees. Bake 1 hour or until onion is tender and can be easily pierced with kitchen fork. Remove veal from milk and cut into pieces approximately 2 inches square. Sprinkle with salt, pepper, and oregano. Beat eggs with 1 tablespoon oil. Dip veal into eggs, then in bread crumbs, patting crumbs into meat to make firm coating. Heat ¼ inch oil in electric skillet preheated at 370 degrees. Sauté veal until medium brown on both sides. Peel onion, cut in half through stem end, and cut crosswise into thinnest possible slices. Break slices apart to make strips. Mix onions in bowl with 2 tablespoons oil, vinegar, and anchovies. Season with salt and pepper. Slice tomatoes thin. Cut buns in half lengthwise and spread with butter. Place veal on bun bottoms. Place onions on veal. Place sliced tomatoes on onions. Place bun tops in position and fasten with toothpicks to hold in place. Wrap sandwiches individually with clear plastic wrap. Chill.

❡ Preheat oven at 375 degrees. Remove plastic wrap from sandwiches, place on shallow baking pan or cookie sheet, and bake 10 to 12 minutes.

Polish Sausage and Kraut Heroes

8 hero buns or large club rolls
Soft butter or margarine
2 pounds Polish sausage (kielbasi)
1 pound sauerkraut, drained
2 tablespoons salad oil
½ cup green pepper cut in very thin strips
½ cup onion cut in very thin strips
½ cup catsup
2 tablespoons sugar
2 tablespoons cider vinegar
Salt
Pepper

Place sausage in boiling water, cutting in half crosswise if necessary to fit pot. Simmer for 20 minutes. Remove casing from sausage with paring knife. Heat salad oil in a saucepan and add green pepper and onion. Sauté, stirring constantly, until onion is limp, but not browned. Combine onion mixture with sauerkraut, catsup, sugar, and vinegar. Add salt and pepper if desired. Cut sausage crosswise into slices ¼ inch thick. Cut buns in half lengthwise. Remove by scraping about ½ inch of the soft centers of the bottom halves of buns. Spread buns with butter. Place sausage slices on bun bottoms. Spoon sauerkraut mixture on top of sausage, spreading it evenly. Cover with bun tops. Place filled buns in shallow pans. Chill.

❮ Preheat oven at 400 degrees. Bake buns 12 to 15 minutes or until heated through.

Triple Deck Tongue, Swiss Cheese, and Egg Salad Sandwiches

24 thin slices white sandwich bread
Soft butter or margarine
8 hard-boiled eggs
½ cup mayonnaise
2 teaspoons prepared mustard
¼ cup capers in vinegar, drained
Salt
White pepper
1 pound cooked smoked beef tongue, thinly sliced
½ pound Swiss emmentaler cheese, thinly sliced
2 cups medium cream sauce (see page 50)
¼ pound process swiss cheese, shredded
Cayenne pepper
8 tablespoons melted butter or margarine

Chop eggs finely as for egg salad. Mix eggs with mayonnaise, mustard, and capers. Season to taste with salt and pepper. Spread bread with soft butter. Spread one slice of bread with egg mixture. Place second slice of bread on top. Place tongue and emmentaler cheese on top, keeping slices within margin of bread. Place third slice of bread, buttered side down, on top of tongue and cheese. Press gently. Continue in this manner until 8 sandwiches are assembled. Crust may be left on or sliced off with very sharp knife. Wrap each sandwich individually in clear plastic wrap. Chill. Heat cream sauce with process cheese until cheese melts. Add a dash of cayenne pepper. Chill.   •

❡ Preheat oven at 450 degrees. Remove plastic wrap and place sandwiches on a cookie sheet. Brush top of each sandwich with melted butter. Bake 10 to 15 minutes or until sandwiches are lightly browned on top. Reheat sauce, thinning with milk or cream if desired. Pour sauce over sandwiches on serving plates or pass separately at table.

Triple Deck Corned Beef Salad, Bacon, and Caraway Cheese Sandwiches

24 thin slices white sandwich bread
Soft butter or margarine
24 slices bacon, fried crisp and drained
½ pound caraway cheese, thinly sliced
1 pound cooked corned beef, brisket or round, thinly sliced
½ cup finely chopped dill pickle
½ cup mayonnaise
1 teaspoon prepared mustard
2 cups unseasoned medium cream sauce (see page 50)
1 tablespoon very finely minced fresh dill
½ teaspoon dill salt
Pepper
8 tablespoons melted butter or margarine

Cut corned beef into very small dice and mix with pickle, mayonnaise, and mustard. Spread bread with soft butter. Spread one slice of bread with corned beef mixture. Place second slice of bread on top. Place bacon and caraway cheese on top, keeping within margin of bread. Cut or fold bacon and cheese slices if necessary. Place third slice of bread, buttered side down, on top of bacon and cheese. Press gently. Continue in this manner until 8 sandwiches are assembled. Crust may be left on or sliced off with very sharp knife. Wrap each sandwich individually in clear plastic wrap. Chill. Season cream sauce with fresh dill and dill salt. Add pepper to taste.

❰ Preheat oven at 450 degrees. Remove plastic wrap and place sandwiches on cookie sheet. Brush top of each sandwich with melted butter. Bake 10 to 12 minutes or until sandwiches are lightly browned on top. Reheat sauce while sandwiches are baking. Thin sauce with milk or cream if desired. Pour over sandwiches or pass separately at table.

Triple Deck Turkey, Ham, and Roasted Pepper Sandwiches

24 thin slices white sandwich bread
Soft butter or margarine
¾ pound Virginia style baked ham, thinly sliced
13 ounce jar roasted sweet peppers, drained
1 pound cooked turkey breast or turkey roll, thinly sliced
½ cup mayonnaise
2 cups medium cream sauce (see page 50)
3 ounces Roquefort or blue cheese, crumbled
1 small onion, grated
8 tablespoons melted butter or margarine

Spread bread with soft butter. Place sliced ham and peppers on one slice of bread, keeping ham and peppers within margin of bread. Place second slice of bread on top. Place sliced turkey within margin of bread. Spread mayonnaise on turkey. Place third slice of bread, buttered side down, on turkey. Press gently. Continue in this manner until 8 sandwiches are assembled. Crust may be left on or sliced off with very sharp knife. Wrap each sandwich individually in clear plastic wrap. Chill. Mix cheese and grated onion into cream sauce. Chill.

❡ Preheat oven at 450 degrees. Remove plastic wrap and place sandwiches on a cookie sheet. Brush top of each sandwich with melted butter. Bake 10 to 12 minutes or until sandwiches are lightly browned on top. Reheat sauce while sandwiches are baking. Thin sauce with milk or cream if desired. Pour over sandwiches or pass separately at table.

Triple Deck Clam and Ham Sandwiches

24 thin slices white sandwich bread
Soft butter or margarine
2 cans (10 ounces each) baby clams, drained
¼ cup mayonnaise
¼ cup finely chopped celery
1 teaspoon lemon juice
1 pound boiled or baked ham, thinly sliced
1 pound firm ripe tomatoes, thinly sliced
2 cups medium cream sauce (see page 50)
2 teaspoons finely minced fresh chives
Salt
Pepper
8 tablespoons melted butter or margarine

Chop clams fine. Combine clams with mayonnaise, celery, and lemon juice. Season to taste with salt and pepper. Spread bread with soft butter. Spread clam mixture on one slice bread. Place second slice on top. Place ham and tomatoes on second slice of bread, keeping both within bread margin. Sprinkle tomatoes with salt and pepper. Continue in this manner until 8 sandwiches are assembled. Crust may be left on or sliced off with very sharp knife. Wrap each sandwich individually with clear plastic wrap. Chill. Mix cream sauce with chives. Chill.

❡ Preheat oven at 450 degrees. Remove plastic wrap and place sandwiches on a cookie sheet. Brush each sandwich on top with melted butter. Bake 10 to 12 minutes or until sandwiches are lightly browned on top. Reheat sauce while sandwiches are baking. Thin with milk or cream if desired. Pour over sandwiches or pass separately at table.

Triple Deck Crab Meat and Canadian Bacon Sandwiches

24 thin slices white sandwich bread
Soft butter or margarine
1 pound sliced Canadian bacon, fully cooked
1 pound fresh deluxe crab lump or 2 cans (7¾ ounces each) fancy crab meat
6 tablespoons finely minced scallions, white and firm part of green
6 tablespoons finely minced green pepper
½ cup mayonnaise
1 teaspoon Dijon mustard
1 teaspoon prepared hot mustard
2 teaspoons horseradish
2 teaspoons lemon juice
Salt
Pepper
2 cups medium cream sauce (see page 50)
1 hard-boiled egg, chopped fine
8 tablespoons melted butter or margarine

Examine crab meat carefully and remove any cartilage or shell. Break crab lump into flakes. Mix crab meat with scallions, green pepper, mayonnaise, both kinds of mustard, horseradish, and lemon juice. Add salt and pepper to taste. Spread bread with soft butter. Spread one slice of bread with crab meat mixture. Place second slice on top. Place Canadian bacon within margin of bread. Place third slice of bread, buttered side down, on top of Canadian bacon. Press gently. Continue in this manner until 8 sandwiches are assembled. Crust may be left on or sliced off with very sharp knife. Wrap each sandwich individually with clear plastic wrap. Chill. Combine hard-boiled egg and cream sauce. Chill.

❧ Preheat oven at 450 degrees. Remove plastic wrap and place sandwiches on a cookie sheet. Brush each sandwich on top with melted butter. Bake 10 to 12 minutes or until sandwiches are lightly browned on top. Reheat sauce while sandwiches are baking. Pour sauce over sandwiches or pass separately at table.

French Toasted Egg and Smoked Salmon Sandwiches

16 slices thin white sandwich bread or rye bread of same size
Soft butter or margarine
8 hard-boiled eggs
½ pound smoked salmon, thinly sliced
1 cup thick cream sauce (see page 50)
1 medium-size onion, grated
2 teaspoons lemon juice
Salt
Pepper
4 eggs, slightly beaten
½ cup light cream or milk
Salad oil

Spread bread generously with soft butter. Chop hard-boiled eggs fine. Cut smoked salmon into ⅛ inch squares. Mix chopped eggs with smoked salmon, cream sauce, grated onion, and lemon juice. Add salt and pepper to taste. Spread salmon mixture on 8 slices bread. Put bread slices together to make sandwiches. Do not let filling ooze out of sides of sandwiches. Press lightly. Mix beaten eggs and cream. Heat ¼ inch oil in electric skillet preheated at 370 degrees. Holding each sandwich firmly with two hands, dip briefly into egg mixture as in making French toast. Sauté sandwiches until medium brown on both sides. Place sandwiches on a lightly greased shallow pan or cookie sheet and cover with clear plastic wrap. Chill.

❡ Preheat oven at 350 degrees. Bake sandwiches 10 to 12 minutes.

French Toasted Ham, Cheese, and Sliced Egg Sandwiches

16 slices thin white sandwich bread
Soft butter or margarine
½ pound boiled ham, sliced thin
½ cup green peppers sliced very fine
1 cup thick cream sauce (see page 50)
¼ pound gruyère cheese, shredded
1 small onion, grated
8 hard-boiled eggs, sliced
Salt
Pepper
4 eggs, slightly beaten
½ cup light cream or milk
Salad oil

Spread bread generously with butter. Cut ham into ⅛ inch squares. Mix ham, green peppers, cream sauce, cheese, and grated onion. Heat over very low flame or in double boiler only until cheese melts. Add salt and pepper to taste. Let ham mixture cool slightly. Spoon ham mixture over bread. Place sliced hard-boiled eggs on top. Sprinkle with salt and pepper. Put bread slices together to make sandwiches. Press lightly but do not let filling ooze out of sides of sandwiches. Heat ¼ inch salad oil in electric skillet preheated at 370 degrees. Mix beaten eggs with cream. Holding each sandwich firmly with two hands, dip briefly into egg mixture as in making French toast. Sauté sandwiches until medium brown on both sides. Place sandwiches on a lightly greased shallow pan or cookie sheet and cover with clear plastic wrap. Chill.

❡ Preheat oven at 350 degrees. Unwrap sandwiches and bake 10 to 12 minutes.

French Toasted Deviled Ham Sandwiches

16 slices thin white sandwich bread or whole wheat bread of same size
Soft butter or margarine
1 pound Virginia style baked ham, thinly sliced
1 cup thick cream sauce (see page 50)
1 medium-size onion, grated
2 teaspoons worcestershire sauce
1 teaspoon bottled sauce diable
1 tablespoon prepared horseradish
Salt
Pepper
Cayenne pepper
4 eggs, slightly beaten
½ cup light cream or milk
Salad oil

Spread bread generously with soft butter. Cut ham into ⅛ inch squares. Mix ham, cream sauce, onion, worcestershire sauce, sauce diable, and horseradish. Add salt, pepper, and a dash of cayenne. Spread ham mixture on bread. Put bread slices together to make sandwiches. Press lightly but do not let filling ooze out of sides of sandwiches. Heat ¼ inch salad oil in electric skillet preheated at 370 degrees. Mix beaten eggs with cream. Holding each sandwich firmly with two hands, dip briefly into egg mixture as in making French toast. Sauté sandwiches until medium brown on both sides. Place sandwiches on a lightly greased shallow pan or cookie sheet and cover with clear plastic wrap. Chill.

❡   Preheat oven at 350 degrees. Unwrap sandwiches and bake 10 to 12 minutes.

French Toasted Chicken and Parmesan Cheese Sandwiches

16 slices thin white sandwich bread
Soft butter or margarine
1 pound chicken roll or cooked chicken or turkey, thinly sliced
Salt
Pepper
4 ounces parmesan cheese, freshly grated
½ cup mayonnaise
2 egg yolks
4 eggs, slightly beaten
½ cup light cream or milk
Salad oil

Spread bread generously with soft butter. Place chicken or turkey on 8 slices of bread, keeping it within margin of bread. Sprinkle with salt and pepper. Mix cheese, mayonnaise, and egg yolks. Spread on remaining slices of bread. Put bread slices together to make sandwiches. Press lightly. Mix beaten eggs and cream. Heat ¼ inch salad oil in electric skillet preheated at 370 degrees. Holding each sandwich firmly with two hands, dip briefly into egg mixture as in making French toast. Sauté sandwiches until medium brown on both sides. Place sandwiches on a lightly greased shallow pan or cookie sheet and cover with clear plastic wrap. Chill.

❦ Preheat oven at 350 degrees. Unwrap sandwiches and bake 10 to 12 minutes.

French Toasted Mortadella, Salami, and Artichoke Sandwiches

16 slices thin white sandwich bread
Soft butter or margarine
1 pound mortadella sausage, thinly sliced
½ pound genoa salami, thinly sliced
6 ounce jar artichoke hearts in oil
4 eggs, slightly beaten
½ cup light cream or milk
Salad oil

Spread 8 slices of bread generously with soft butter. Place mortadella and salami on buttered bread. Meat should not extend beyond margin of bread. Drain artichoke hearts, reserving oil. Cut artichoke hearts into thin slices and place them on meat. Brush remaining bread with oil from artichoke hearts. Put bread slices together to make sandwiches. Press lightly. Mix eggs and cream. Heat ¼ inch salad oil in electric skillet preheated at 370 degrees. Holding each sandwich firmly with two hands, dip into egg mixture briefly as in making French toast. Sauté sandwiches until medium brown on both sides. Place sandwiches on a lightly greased shallow pan or cookie sheet and cover with clear plastic wrap. Chill.

❑ Preheat oven at 350 degrees. Unwrap sandwiches and bake 10 to 12 minutes.

Cream Sauce

Although it appears in countless cookbooks because its uses are countless, and although it is often berated as not worthy of a sophisticated cook's attention, cream sauce is still an essential component of dishes old and new. In a professional kitchen, it is the first job in the morning performed by the highest-ranking cook or *saucier*. The ingredients are standard, but small steps in the procedure often bedevil homemakers. The following procedure should result in a smooth glossy sauce that has a creamlike quality although it is made from milk.

Medium Cream Sauce   1 Cup

2 tablespoons butter, margarine, or shortening
2 tablespoons all-purpose flour
1 cup milk
Salt
White Pepper

Use a small saucepan for the quantity above. Increase size of pan for larger quantities of sauce. Melt butter over very low flame; butter should not sizzle. Remove pan from flame and stir in flour. (Use a wire whip for all stirring. A flat wire whip is best for getting into corners of pan. A larger, balloon-shaped wire whip is more efficient for larger quantities of sauce.) Stir in flour until no dry flour and no lumps remain. In another saucepan bring milk up to a boil but do not boil. Add milk in small batches at a time, stirring well after each addition. When all milk has been added, return pan to a moderate flame and cook, stirring constantly, scraping bottom and corners of pan from time to time, until sauce bubbles. At this point the sauce will have the taste of raw flour. Reduce flame and simmer, stirring occasionally, about 5 minutes or until raw flour taste disappears. Season to taste with salt and pepper. At least ¼ teaspoon salt will be necessary. Cover pan at once with tight lid to keep skin from forming on top. If sauce is to be held a long time, a small quantity of melted butter may be sprinkled on top to prevent skin from forming.

Instant dissolving flour may be used. Do not heat milk or melt butter. Stir flour into cold milk in pan until flour is completely dissolved. Add cold butter and cook over a moderate flame until sauce is thick. Continue cooking as above.

Thin Cream Sauce. Reduce flour and butter to 1 tablespoon each.

Thick Cream Sauce. Increase flour and butter to 4 tablespoons each.

Rich Cream Sauce. Instead of 1 cup milk use ¾ cup milk and ¼ cup light cream.

4

〰

Hot Cheese

PEOPLE LOVE to compare cheeses, especially when a sumptuous cheese platter is set on the table at the end of a dinner. But when, late at night, you serve a hot cheese dish like a welsh rabbit rich with cream and brown ale, comparisons become picayune. One devours spiedini—skewered mozzarella between oven-toasted chunks of bread, doused with hot anchovy sauce—not because of what the man across the table or the lady on the left thinks of it, but for its own mellow, completely absorbing sensation in the mouth. Theoretically, it would be quite possible for you to serve supper guests a different hot cheese dish for at least 365 midnights in a row. The eighteen basic families of cheese branch out into hundreds of magnificent specimens, all candidates for parties. When using the recipes here, don't hesitate to create your own variations with similar cheeses, to substitute tilsiter for Monterey jack, or stuff apricots with gorgonzola instead of pears with Roquefort.

A hot cheese dish such as a fragrant coquille of cheddar and smoked oysters is the tip-off to tall drafts of beer, ale, or stout. Salads are next of kin to cheese, and guests always welcome a great glass bowl filled with crisp greens in a somewhat tart olive oil dressing or a finely shredded coleslaw in a mustard cream dressing. For dessert, any fresh fruit tart, like apple, pear, or blueberry, will strike the perfect chord.

BUYING CHEESE The choicest cheeses are to be found in a cheese specialty shop or the cheese section of a gourmet food shop. You may have to travel farther than the supermarket around the corner, but the extra legwork is always repaid in party pleasure. Remember also that a supermarket cheese shelf won't be able to tell you whether the sliced provolone you're considering is sharp or mild and can't give you a sliver of edam to taste for ripeness. Some cheese specialty shops offer the boon of cheeses freshly shredded upon order for fondues, welsh rabbits, and other party dishes, a labor saver well worth the small added price.

GRATING AND SHREDDING CHEESE If you buy bulk cheese for grating (and you should for its vastly superior flavor), it isn't necessary to work your fingers to the bone, provided you use the proper technique. Hard cheese like parmesan may be grated in a cylinder-type cheese grater turned by hand or electrically, or in an electric blender. If you use a metal grater, the wider the grating surface of the cheese and the bigger each swipe, the faster the job. To shred rather than grate cheese, use the large holes of a metal grater or, more easily, a meat grinder with the fine blade. If you buy sliced cheese and the recipe calls for shredding it, the best procedure is to cut the cheese into very small squares with a heavy French knife.

SLICING CHEESE The best device for slicing is a wire cheese slicer, especially one that can be set for slices of different thicknesses. The Danish-type cheese slicer with its built-in blade cuts slices that are usually too thin for cooking. It's a fine gadget at the cocktail table, but rather laborious in the kitchen. If you use a knife for slicing, be sure it's a very sharp French knife and dip it in very hot water before each cut.

COOKING TEMPERATURES FOR CHEESE Play it cool for hot cheese dishes. A moderate or low oven, or a modest flame under the chafing dish, will melt cheese slowly and deliciously. The heat of a fierce broiler flame only a few inches away will turn most cheeses into stubborn tough strands.

AGE VERSUS YOUTH IN CHEESE Fresh soft cheeses like ricotta are best when, like milk, they're fresh from the dairy. Unaged semisoft cheeses like mozzarella should never be more than a week old. Cheeses that aren't hard but need age, such as port salut, should be ripened till their flavor is rich and mellow but not sharp. Hard cheeses like cheddar and very hard cheeses like parmesan should be completely matured when you buy them, but must not be kept in your refrigerator until they're wizened with old age.

SLICED PACKAGED VERSUS BULK CHEESE   For party purposes, bulk cheese bought from a knowledgeable merchant and sliced by him to order is far and away the best answer.

CHEESE AND BREAD   Many cheese recipes call for sliced sandwich bread as one of the main ingredients. American firm white sandwich bread, in square loaves, should be a day or two old for best results. The best bread for flavor and texture is white Italian or French bread, but the irregular shape of the loaves makes it necessary for the homemaker to use careful judgment if she is substituting either for the conventional American loaf.

Cheese Coquilles with Smoked Oysters

1 pound aged cheddar cheese,
  shredded
3 cans (3⅔ ounces each) smoked
  oysters, drained
4 cups white bread crumbs
1 quart milk

4 eggs, beaten
2 teaspoons salt
½ cup white bread crumbs
½ cup freshly grated parmesan
  cheese
Paprika

In mixing bowl combine 4 cups bread crumbs, milk, eggs, salt, and cheddar cheese, blending thoroughly. Divide oysters among 16 coquille shells that hold half a cup each, or among 8 shirred egg dishes if coquille shells of this size are not available. Spoon cheese mixture over oysters. Sprinkle with ½ cup bread crumbs and parmesan cheese. Sprinkle lightly with paprika. Chill.

❆ Preheat oven at 375 degrees. Bake 20 to 25 minutes or until lightly browned.

Croûtes with Münster Cheese and Curried Shrimp

1 pound (cooked weight) boiled, shelled, and deveined shrimp
  (2 pounds raw shrimp)
1½ pounds thinly sliced münster cheese, preferably Danish,
    although domestic may be used
16 slices firm white sandwich bread
2 cups milk
4 tablespoons instant dissolving flour
4 tablespoons butter or margarine
1 tablespoon curry powder
2 tablespoons Amontillado sherry
Salt
Pepper
6 ounces butter at room temperature or soft margarine

Cut shrimp in half lengthwise. Pour milk into saucepan. Stir in flour until flour dissolves. Add 4 tablespoons butter or margarine. Cook over a moderate flame, stirring constantly, until sauce is thick. Mix curry powder and sherry, blending well, and add to sauce. Simmer 5 minutes, stirring occasionally. Add salt and pepper to taste. Toast bread under broiler on one side only. Spread untoasted side with 6 ounces butter. Place half the cheese on the bread. Place shrimp, cut side down, on cheese. Spoon sauce over shrimp. Place balance of cheese on top. Place croûtes on cookie sheets or shallow baking pans. Cover with clear plastic wrap. Chill.

❡ Preheat oven at 350 degrees. Remove plastic wrap and bake 15 to 18 minutes.

Edam Cheese Croûtes with Roquefort-Stuffed Pear

16 slices firm white sandwich bread
8 ounces Roquefort cheese
½ pound butter at room temperature or soft margarine
2 tablespoons heavy sweet cream
16 medium-size canned Bartlett pear halves, drained
1 pound baked or boiled ham, thinly sliced
1 pound edam cheese, thinly sliced

Break up Roquefort cheese with fork. Add 2 ounces butter and heavy cream. Work mixture smooth. Place mixture inside hollow of each pear. Toast bread under broiler on one side only. Spread untoasted side with butter or margarine. Arrange ham slices on bread. On each slice of bread place a pear, stuffed side down. Place slice of edam cheese on top of pear; part of pear may be exposed. Place croûtes on cookie sheets or shallow baking pans. Cover with clear plastic wrap. Chill.

❡ Preheat oven at 350 degrees. Remove plastic wrap and bake 15 minutes or until cheese is soft.

Croûtes with Smoked Cheese and Tongue

1 pound smoked cheddar cheese, shredded
1 pound cooked corned beef tongue, thinly sliced
16 slices firm white sandwich bread
3 cups milk
6 tablespoons instant dissolving flour
6 tablespoons butter or margarine
3 egg yolks, beaten slightly
Salt
Pepper
Paprika
8 ounce can tomato sauce

Cut tongue into ¼ inch squares. Pour milk into saucepan. Stir in flour until flour dissolves. Add butter or margarine. Cook over a moderate flame, stirring constantly, until sauce is thick. Simmer 5 minutes, stirring occasionally. Add 3 tablespoons sauce to egg yolks, stirring well. Add yolks to sauce and simmer 1 minute, stirring constantly. Add salt and pepper to taste. Stir cheese and tongue into sauce. Toast bread under broiler on one side only. Spoon sauce mixture, spreading evenly, over untoasted side of bread. Place bread on cookie sheets or shallow baking pans. Cover with clear plastic wrap. Chill.

❬ Preheat broiler. Sprinkle croûtes lightly with paprika. Drizzle a few light lines or "threads" of tomato sauce on croûtes. Broil until croûtes turn a light mottled brown.

Croûtes with Monterey Jack Cheese and Apple

1½ pounds thinly sliced Monterey jack cheese
4 medium-size delicious apples
16 slices firm white sandwich bread
Salad oil
Flour
6 ounce package sliced almonds
Salt
6 ounces butter at room temperature or soft margarine

Peel and core apples. Cut each into 12 slices. Heat ⅛ inch oil in electric skillet preheated at 370 degrees. Dip apple slices in flour; shake off excess flour. Sauté until tender. During sautéing wipe pan clean and replace with fresh oil as necessary. Preheat oven at 350 degrees. Mix almonds with 1 tablespoon oil and sprinkle lightly with salt. Spread almonds on shallow baking pan and bake about 10 minutes, or until almonds are light brown. Avoid scorching. Toast bread under broiler on one side only. Spread untoasted side with butter. Place half the cheese on buttered side of bread. Place apples on cheese. Top with balance of cheese. Sprinkle with almonds. Place on cookie sheet or shallow baking pan. Cover with clear plastic wrap. Chill.

❡ Preheat oven at 350 degrees. Remove plastic wrap and bake about 15 minutes, or until cheese melts.

Croûtes with Brick Cheese and Onion

1 pound brick cheese, shredded
½ pound ricotta cheese
16 slices firm white sandwich bread
2 tablespoons salad oil
2 tablespoons butter
2 cups onions cut in ¼ inch dice
⅓ cup mayonnaise
2 large cloves garlic
Salt
Pepper
6 ounces butter at room temperature or soft margarine
Grated parmesan cheese
Paprika

Toast bread under broiler on one side only. Heat oil and 2 tablespoons butter in saucepan over low flame. Add onions and sauté, stirring frequently, until onions are soft but not browned. Remove from flame. In mixing bowl combine onions, brick cheese, ricotta cheese, and mayonnaise. Force garlic through garlic press into bowl. Stir well. Add salt and pepper to taste. Spread untoasted side of bread with 6 ounces butter or margarine. Spread cheese mixture on bread, coating it completely to edge. Sprinkle with grated cheese. Sprinkle lightly with paprika. Place croûtes on cookie sheets or shallow baking pans. Cover with clear plastic wrap. Chill.

❡ Preheat oven at 400 degrees. Unwrap croûtes and bake 10 to 12 minutes. Place under broiler flame if additional browning is desired, watching constantly to prevent scorching.

Croque-Monsieur

1 pound Swiss emmentaler cheese or natural gruyère cheese, thinly sliced
½ pound cooked or canned ham, thinly sliced
16 slices firm white sandwich bread
6 ounces butter at room temperature or soft margarine
Dijon or Düsseldorf mustard
3 eggs
¾ cup light cream
¼ teaspoon salt
¼ teaspoon paprika
Salad oil

Spread bread with butter or margarine. On half the slices place the cheese and ham. Spread lightly with mustard. Cover with top slice of bread to make sandwiches. Press slightly. Beat eggs, cream, salt, and paprika until well blended. Heat ⅛ inch oil in electric skillet preheated at 370 degrees. Dip sandwiches lightly into egg mixture; they should not be held in mixture until they are too soft to handle. Sauté sandwiches in skillet until they are medium brown on both sides. Add more oil to pan if necessary during sautéing. Place sandwiches on cookie sheets or shallow baking pans. Cover with clear plastic wrap. Chill.

❡ Preheat oven at 375 degrees. Remove plastic wrap and bake 12 to 15 minutes.

Croque-Monsieur with Chicken   Substitute sliced chicken or chicken roll for ham.

Phyllo Pie with Ricotta and Ham

18 phyllo leaves
1 pound ricotta cheese
¼ pound feta cheese (washed in cold water if salty)
¼ pound melted butter
4 eggs, beaten
1 tablespoon finely minced fresh chives or scallions
1 medium-size onion, grated
1 teaspoon dillweed
6 ounces thinly sliced ham, cut in ¼ inch squares
Salt
Pepper

Prepared phyllo pastry leaves, available at Middle Eastern or specialty food shops, are extremely tender and delicious but tend to break up if not properly handled. Be sure phyllo leaves are out of refrigerator at least 2 hours before using. Remove leaves from package and spread them on working surface. Cover leaves with a damp cloth and keep them away from drafts. Separate one leaf very carefully from the next, using two hands to lift and fold leaves, and keep leaves covered as much as possible during preparation of dish.

Grease two 7-by-11-inch shallow pans with butter. Break up feta cheese with fork or chop with knife into small pieces. Mix ricotta cheese, feta cheese, eggs, chives or scallions, onion, dillweed, and ham. Season with salt and pepper. Place a folded phyllo leaf in pan and brush lightly with butter. Add 4 more leaves, brushing each with butter after it is placed in pan. Spread half the cheese mixture on top leaves. Add 4 more folded leaves, each brushed with butter. Prepare second pan in same manner. Cover with clear plastic wrap. Chill.

❦ Preheat oven at 375 degrees. Remove plastic wrap and bake 30 minutes or until golden brown. Cut each pie into 8 squares.

Phyllo Pie with Ricotta and Spinach

18 phyllo leaves
1 pound ricotta cheese
¼ pound feta cheese (washed in cold water if salty)
¼ pound melted butter
1 cup milk
2 tablespoons instant dissolving flour
2 tablespoons butter
2 eggs, beaten
10 ounce package frozen chopped spinach, cooked and pressed dry
1 medium-size onion, grated
¼ cup white bread crumbs
Salt
Pepper
⅛ teaspoon freshly grated nutmeg

Follow instructions in previous recipe for handling phyllo leaves. Grease two 7-by-11-inch shallow pans with melted butter. Break up feta cheese with fork or chop with knife into small pieces. In saucepan stir flour into milk until flour is completely dissolved. Add 2 tablespoons butter. Cook over a moderate flame, stirring constantly until sauce is thick. Simmer 5 minutes, stirring occasionally. Mix sauce with cheeses, eggs, spinach, onion, and bread crumbs. Add salt and pepper to taste and nutmeg. Place a folded phyllo leaf in pan and brush lightly with melted butter. Add 4 more leaves, brushing each with butter. Spread half the cheese mixture on top leaves. Add 4 more folded leaves, each brushed with butter. Prepare second pan in same manner. Cover with clear plastic wrap. Chill.

❧ Preheat oven at 375 degrees. Remove plastic wrap and bake 30 minutes or until golden brown. Cut each pie into 8 squares.

Port Salut and Ham Rolls

8 hard round dinner rolls, about 3½ to 4 inches in diameter
1½ cups onions, cut in ½ inch dice
8 ounces butter at room temperature or soft margarine
¾ pound sliced boiled or baked ham
1½ pounds port salut cheese, sliced
2 cans (4 ounces each) sliced mushrooms, drained
10½ ounce can undiluted golden mushroom soup
¼ teaspoon dillweed
⅛ teaspoon leaf thyme
Salt
Pepper

Sauté onions in 2 tablespoons butter until onions are barely tender. Cut ham in ½ inch squares. Cut half the cheese in ½ inch squares. Cut balance of cheese crosswise in strips ½ inch wide. Cut rolls in half crosswise and scoop out enough crumbs so that rolls form cups. Brush inside of rolls with balance of butter. In a mixing bowl combine onions, ham, cheese squares, mushrooms, mushroom soup, dillweed, and thyme. Season with salt and pepper. Pile mixture into rolls. Place cheese strips across each mound of filling. Place rolls in a shallow baking pan. Cover with clear plastic wrap. Chill.

❡ Preheat oven at 350 degrees. Remove plastic wrap and bake rolls 15 to 18 minutes.

Cheese Beignets with Bacon and Remoulade Sauce

1 cup water
¼ cup butter
½ teaspoon salt
1½ cups all-purpose flour
5 eggs, unbeaten
8 ounces cantal cheese, shredded
⅓ cup grated parmesan cheese
Salad oil

2 pounds sliced bacon
2 cups mayonnaise
2 teaspoons finely minced fresh chives
2 teaspoons anchovy paste
¼ cup finely minced sour gherkins
2 teaspoons Dijon mustard
2 tablespoons capers in vinegar,
    drained and coarsely chopped

Heat water, butter, and salt in heavy saucepan until butter melts. Remove from fire. Add flour all at once and stir well until all ingredients hold together in one mass. Some muscle power will be required for this step. Tranfer mixture to electric mixer. Add eggs one at a time, running mixer at slowest speed to keep batter inside bowl. After last egg has been added, beat mixture at medium speed 3 to 4 minutes. Add both kinds of cheese, mixing well. Heat salad oil to a depth of ½ inch in electric skillet preheated at 370 degrees. Lower batter by heaping teaspoonfuls into pan. Fry, turning once, until well browned on two sides. Drain on paper toweling. Chill. This type of fritter will not become soggy when reheated. Sauté or bake bacon until half-done. Remove from fat. Chill. Stir together mayonnaise, chives, anchovy paste, gherkins, mustard, and capers. Chill.

❡ Preheat oven at 400 degrees. Place beignets on shallow baking pan or cookie sheet. Heat 10 to 15 minutes. Place bacon in oven at same time and heat until well-done. Serve with remoulade sauce.

Cheese Tart with Anchovies   2 tarts, 8 to 12 portions

2 nine-inch unbaked pie crusts
2 tablespoons salad oil
1 cup onion cut in $\frac{1}{4}$ inch dice
$\frac{1}{2}$ cup green pepper cut in $\frac{1}{4}$ inch dice
2 pounds ricotta cheese
$\frac{1}{2}$ pound Bel Paese cheese, shredded
4 ounces Swiss emmentaler cheese, shredded
6 eggs, beaten
1 cup milk
$\frac{1}{4}$ teaspoon oregano
1 teaspoon salt
$\frac{1}{4}$ teaspoon ground white pepper
12 anchovies in oil, drained
Paprika

Preheat oven at 400 degrees. Sauté onion and green pepper in oil only until vegetables begin to soften. They should not be browned. Mix thoroughly the three kinds of cheese, eggs, milk, oregano, salt, pepper, and sautéed vegetables. Turn into prepared pie shells. Arrange anchovies on top of filling. Sprinkle lightly with paprika. Bake 10 minutes. Reduce heat to 325 degrees. Bake 25 to 35 minutes longer, or until filling is firm when lightly touched. Chill.

❡ Preheat oven at 375 degrees. Bake tarts 20 to 25 minutes.

Fried Caraway Cheese Sandwiches

16 slices firm white sandwich bread
6 ounces butter at room temperature
1½ pounds caraway cheese, sliced
½ cup canned tomato sauce
½ cup sour cream
1 teaspoon grated onion
¼ teaspoon leaf thyme
1 cup milk
3 eggs beaten with ¼ cup milk
Toasted bread crumbs
Salad oil

Spread each slice of bread with butter. Place half the cheese slices on 8 slices of bread. Cheese slices should be slightly smaller than bread; if cheese extends to rim of bread, it may ooze out during cooking. Mix tomato sauce, sour cream, onion, and thyme. Spread tomato mixture over the 8 slices of cheese-covered bread. Place balance of cheese on top. Place remaining bread, buttered side down, on top to make sandwiches. Press slightly. Holding sandwiches firmly, dip quickly in milk only long enough to moisten bread. Dip in beaten eggs. Dip in bread crumbs, coating top, bottom, and sides of sandwiches thoroughly. Preheat ¼ inch oil in electric skillet at 370 degrees. Fry sandwiches, turning once, until light brown on both sides. Place sandwiches on cookie sheet or shallow baking pan. Cover with clear plastic wrap. Chill.

❑ Preheat oven at 375 degrees. Remove plastic wrap and bake sandwiches 15 to 18 minutes.

Open Cream Provolone Sandwiches

16 slices firm white sandwich bread
1 cup milk
3 eggs beaten with ¼ cup milk
Toasted bread crumbs
Salad oil
1 pound cream cheese
1 tablespoon finely minced fresh chives
¼ cup heavy cream
12 ounces provolone cheese, sliced
1½ cups canned tomato sauce
¼ teaspoon oregano
1 teaspoon anchovy paste

Dip bread on one side only quickly into milk. Bread should just be moistened, not soggy. Dip same side into beaten egg mixture, then into bread crumbs. Preheat ¼ inch oil in electric skillet set at 370 degrees. Fry bread on coated side only. Discard oil if it becomes discolored, wipe pan clean, and add fresh oil to finish frying. Place bread, fried side down, on cookie sheets or shallow baking pans. Work cream cheese, chives, and cream until well blended and soft enough to spread easily. Add more cream if necessary to make cheese easily spreadable. Spread bread on unfried side with cream cheese. Place a slice of provolone cheese on cream cheese. Cover sandwiches with clear plastic wrap and chill.

❡ Preheat oven at 375 degrees. In a saucepan combine tomato sauce, oregano, and anchovy paste, mixing until completely blended. Heat until sauce bubbles. Unwrap sandwiches and spoon tomato sauce on cheese. Bake sandwiches 12 to 15 minutes.

Skewered Mozzarella (Spiedini) with Anchovy Sauce

16 slices firm white sandwich bread
1½ pounds mozzarella cheese, sliced
¼ pound melted butter
2 ounce can flat filets of anchovies
½ cup olive oil
½ cup finely minced pepperoni (pepper salad in oil)
2 tablespoons red wine vinegar
¼ cup bread crumbs
2 tablespoons capers in vinegar, drained and coarsely chopped

Remove crusts from bread. Cut each slice into 4 squares. Cut mozzarella cheese into 48 squares of same size as bread pieces. Make a stack of alternate slices of bread and cheese, using 4 slices of bread and 3 of cheese to each "sandwich." (Two sandwiches equal 1 portion of spiedini.) Fasten sandwiches with bamboo skewers (cut in half if necessary) or fasten with cocktail spears. Brush end slices of each sandwich with melted butter. Stack spiedini upright in a shallow baking pan. Cover pan completely with clear plastic wrap to keep bread from drying. Chill. Drain anchovies, discarding oil, and chop coarsely. In a saucepan combine anchovies with balance of butter, olive oil, pepperoni, vinegar, bread crumbs, and capers. Chill.

❡ Preheat oven at 350 degrees. Remove plastic wrap from spiedini. Make sure that stacks of bread and cheese are securely upright; use an inverted baking cup or two if necessary to hold them in place, since they tend to topple over during baking. Bake 15 to 20 minutes. Heat sauce over a moderate flame while spiedini are baking. Pass sauce at table. Skewers may be removed from spiedini before serving or at the table.

Cheese and Potato Quiche

1 quart and 1 pint potatoes, peeled and cut in ½ inch thick slices
2 tablespoons butter
2 eggs, beaten
Salt
Pepper
2 cups light cream
4 eggs, beaten
1 pound Swiss emmentaler cheese, shredded
1 pound provolone cheese, shredded
Cayenne pepper
Grated parmesan cheese
Paprika

Boil sliced potatoes in salted water until tender. Drain. Mash potatoes. Add 2 table-spoons butter, stirring until butter melts. Add 2 beaten eggs and salt and pepper to taste, stirring well. Grease two 9-inch pie plates. Spread mashed potatoes evenly on bottom of pie plates. Preheat oven at 350 degrees. Heat cream up to boiling point but do not boil. In a mixing bowl combine cream, 4 beaten eggs, emmentaler and provolone cheese, 1 teaspoon salt, ¼ teaspoon pepper, and dash of cayenne. Spoon mixture on top of potatoes. Sprinkle with parmesan cheese. Sprinkle lightly with paprika. Bake ½ hour or until top is lightly browned. Quiche will rise and then settle after cooling. Chill.

❡ Preheat oven at 350 degrees. Reheat quiche 18 to 20 minutes. Cut into 8 or 12 wedge-shaped portions with pie server.

Welsh Rabbit

2½ pounds aged sharp cheddar cheese, shredded
2 cups light cream
3 tablespoons instant dissolving flour
2 cups dark ale (such as Bass's)
1 teaspoon dry mustard
1 teaspoon prepared mustard
2 teaspoons lemon juice
Cayenne pepper
Salt
Pepper
4 egg yolks, beaten

Pour cream into top part of double boiler. Stir in flour until it is dissolved. Heat over a low direct flame, stirring constantly, until cream is thickened. Place pan over simmering water in bottom section of double boiler. Add ale and both kinds of mustard, stirring well. When mixture is hot, add cheese. Stir occasionally until cheese is melted and blended with other ingredients. Add lemon juice and dash of cayenne. Add salt and pepper to taste. Chill in same pan.

❡ Reheat welsh rabbit over simmering water in bottom section of double boiler. When hot, add several tablespoons of rabbit to egg yolks. Slowly pour yolks into rabbit. Heat 3 to 5 minutes longer. Correct seasoning if necessary. Serve over toast on serving plates, or pour into chafing dish and serve at table with toast.

Welsh Rabbit with French Fried Eggs   Pour 1 inch salad oil into an electric skillet. Just before serving time preheat skillet at 370 degrees. Fry 8 eggs, 4 at a time. On each serving plate place 2 pieces of toast cut diagonally. Place eggs on toast. Spoon welsh rabbit on top.

Welsh Rabbit with Anchovy Toast   Mix ⅓ cup butter at room temperature with 1 tablespoon anchovy paste until well blended. Toast 8 slices of bread on one side only under broiler flame. Spread anchovy butter on untoasted side of each slice. Place 2 anchovy filets diagonally on each slice. Place toast on cookie or baking sheet. Chill. Before serving, place toast in moderate oven preheated at 350 degrees about 5 minutes. Place a slice of anchovy toast on each serving plate. Spoon welsh rabbit on toast.

Welsh Rabbit with Canadian Bacon   Mix 3 tablespoons honey with 3 tablespoons brown sugar until well blended. Brush 24 slices Canadian bacon on both sides with honey mixture. Place on cookie or baking sheet. Before serving, place bacon under a preheated broiler flame 3 to 5 minutes, turning once. On each serving plate, place a slice of toast cut diagonally, topped with 3 slices Canadian bacon. Spoon welsh rabbit on top.

Welsh Rabbit with Fresh Asparagus   Carefully wash 3 pounds fresh asparagus, thick stalks if possible. Break or cut off tough bottom sections and discard. With vegetable peeler cut away scales and stringy surface of each stalk. Boil till tender. Before serving briefly reheat asparagus in water. Drain. Place a slice of toast cut diagonally on each serving plate. Arrange asparagus on top. Spoon welsh rabbit on asparagus.

Swiss Fondue

The usual size of fondue dish accommodates four people spearing bread into it from time to time. At a party of eight, you should have two fondue dishes and the fondue should be made ahead of time, preferably in a large double boiler in the kitchen. At party time the fondue can be transferred to fondue sets over flames at the serving table and simply reheated. The following recipe will not cause the tough strands of cheese that sometimes bedevil fondue hosts.

2½ pounds Swiss emmentaler cheese, shredded
2 large cut cloves of garlic
⅓ cup sweet butter
⅓ cup all-purpose flour
5 cups dry white wine

2 tablespoons lemon juice
⅓ cup kirsch
Grated whole nutmeg
Salt
White pepper

Rub the top section of a double boiler vigorously with garlic. Discard garlic. Melt butter in the top part of the double boiler over a low direct flame. Remove from heat. Stir in flour. In another pan heat wine up to the boiling point. Very slowly stir wine into the flour mixture, stirring constantly. Place wine mixture over simmering water in bottom section of the double boiler. Top pan should not be in actual contact with water. Cook, stirring occasionally, until mixture is thick. Add lemon juice and stir well. Add cheese in small batches, stirring well after each addition until each batch of cheese melts. Stir in kirsch, a dash of nutmeg, and salt and pepper to taste. Chill.

❡ At serving time transfer cheese to fondue pots and heat, stirring occasionally, until cheese is again completely melted. Serve with French bread cut into chunks, each chunk containing a crusty side.

Fondue Gruyère   Imported natural gruyère cheese may be used in place of emmentaler.

Fondue Vermouth   Dry French vermouth may be used in place of white wine, adding a subtle herb flavor.

Fondue Geneva

1 pound natural gruyère cheese, shredded
¾ pound medium-size noodles
¼ cup butter
1 cup toasted bread crumbs
2 teaspoons chopped fresh chives
12 eggs
1 cup light cream
½ pound butter
Salt
White pepper
Cayenne pepper

Boil noodles in salted water, following directions on package, until noodles are just barely tender. Drain, cover with fresh cold water, and chill. Melt ¼ cup butter over low flame. Remove from fire. Stir in bread crumbs and chives. Chill. In top section of double boiler beat eggs until whites are no longer visible. Stir in cream and cheese. Chill.

❡ Preheat oven at 350 degrees. Reheat noodles in water. Drain very well. Turn into shallow casserole. Sprinkle bread crumb mixture on top noodles. Place casserole in oven to keep warm until needed. Place cheese mixture over simmering water in bottom part of double boiler. Break ½ pound butter into small pieces and add to cheese mixture. Heat, stirring frequently, until mixture is thickened and smooth. Add salt and pepper to taste, and dash of cayenne. Turn fondue into serving dish or chafing dish over simmering water. At table, spoon noodles onto serving dishes. Spoon fondue over noodles.

5

~

Seafood

IF YOU COULD always match your guests to your nocturnal menus, you would invite only those with inherently subtle tastes, flexible minds, and a choice sense of humor for a midnight supper of seafood. Fish and shellfish have subtleties that exist even in their raw state, as any lover of oysters or clams on the half shell, or a sushi-eating Japanese, will avow.

Few foods other than seafood depend so completely on their raw quality for successful cooking. In most cases, except when canned or smoked fish is required, the fresher the seafood the better it will be in its finished form. You can judge the quality of a small whole fish rather easily; the eyes are clear, bright, and full, the gills are reddish pink, and the flesh is firm and elastic. But if you're buying a small chunk of a two-hundred-pound tuna or a chunk of a twenty-pound salmon or turbot, these telltale signs are not always evident. Also, many a seafood dish can be made not from raw fish but from fish freshly cooked by the fish merchant, such as boiled, peeled, and deveined shrimp or boiled fresh lobster. Or sometimes the recipe calls for fresh crab lump, which is not cooked by the fish dealer but is purchased by him from a crab processor. These are all magnificent labor savers for the homemaker and are well worth the reasonable extra charge most fish dealers ask. But the only guarantee of the quality of such seafood is the word of a fish merchant you know is dependable from firsthand experience. The least expensive and certainly the least reliable of all seafood is that fund in supermarkets, where fresh fish normally arrives but once a week and where the quality of, say, the frozen peeled shrimp in the frozen-food counters will vary from good to positively inedible.

The greatest sin in seafood cookery is overcooking, and the greatest virtue, therefore, knowing when to stop cooking. Seafood dishes that have been cooked beforehand for a party late at night are reheated to bring them up to warm serving temperature, about 160 degrees in the center of the dish. Such reheating is usually brief, but, because it's brief and dare not be prolonged, the hostess must be especially alert during this last-minute step.

Curried Crab Meat, Peas, and Water Chestnuts

1½ pounds fresh deluxe crab lump or fancy canned crab meat
1½ cups fresh or frozen peas, cooked
8 ounce can water chestnuts, drained and thinly sliced
3 cups milk
6 tablespoons instant dissolving flour
6 tablespoons butter

1 medium-size onion, grated
1 tablespoon curry powder
3 tablespoons light cream
3 tablespoons medium dry sherry
Salt
White pepper

Examine crab meat carefully and remove any shell or cartilage. Pour milk into saucepan and stir in flour until flour dissolves. Add butter. Cook over moderate flame, stirring constantly with wire whip, until sauce thickens. Reduce flame as low as possible and simmer 5 minutes, stirring occasionally. Add grated onion to sauce. Dissolve curry in cream and add to sauce. Add crab meat and water chestnuts. Simmer 10 minutes, stirring frequently. Add sherry, and salt and pepper to taste. Remove from fire and stir in peas. Chill.

❦ Reheat over low flame or double boiler, stirring occasionally. Thin with cream or milk if desired. Correct seasoning if necessary. Serve with rice and chutney.

Curried Crab Lump with Baked Eggplant

1 pound fresh deluxe crab lump or 2 cans (7¾ ounces each) fancy crab meat
16 slices peeled eggplant, ½ inch thick, 3 to 4 inches in diameter
Flour
3 eggs, well beaten
Salad oil
¼ cup sliced scallions
Bread crumbs
½ cup milk
1 cup mayonnaise
2 teaspoons curry powder
Salt
Pepper
¼ cup melted butter

Examine crab meat carefully, breaking apart to remove any pieces of cartilage or shell. Dip eggplant slices in flour to coat completely, then dip in egg. Heat ¼ inch salad oil in skillet. Sauté eggplant until tender. Place eggplant on lightly greased shallow baking pans. Cut scallions, including solid part of green, crosswise into thinnest possible slices. Soak ½ cup bread crumbs with milk. In a large mixing bowl stir the mayonnaise and curry powder. Add softened bread crumbs, crab lump, and scallions. Blend well, adding salt and pepper to taste. Form mounds of crab lump mixture over eggplant. Sprinkle lightly with dry bread crumbs. Chill.

❡ Preheat oven at 375 degrees. Sprinkle crab mounds with melted butter. Bake 20 to 25 minutes.

Coconut Shrimp with Pineapple

2 pounds (cooked weight) shrimp, boiled, shelled, and deveined
  (4 pounds raw shrimp)
20 ounce can pineapple chunks
2 cans (4 ounces each) shredded coconut
3 cups milk
½ cup light cream
6 tablespoons butter
6 tablespoons flour
Salt
Pepper
1 cup prepared Hawaiian coconut chips

Put shredded coconut, milk, and cream in a saucepan. Over a very low flame bring up to the boiling point but do not boil. Remove from fire and let coconut milk remain in saucepan ½ hour. When coconut milk is cool enough to handle, force it through a double thickness of cheesecloth. Discard shredded coconut and return coconut milk to a saucepan. Again bring up to a boil but do not boil. In another saucepan melt 6 tablespoons butter over a low flame. Slowly stir in flour, blending well with a wire whip. Slowly stir in coconut milk, blending well. Bring up to a boil, reduce flame, and simmer 5 minutes, stirring frequently. Add shrimp. Season lightly with salt and pepper. Chill. Drain pineapple well. Chill.

❡ Combine shrimp and drained pineapple. Reheat over moderate flame, stirring frequently, or in top of double boiler. Spoon into a shallow casserole or large au gratin dish. Sprinkle coconut chips on top.

Shrimp and Mushrooms with Horseradish Cream Sauce

2 pounds (cooked weight) shrimp, boiled, shelled and deveined
   (4 pounds raw shrimp)
¾ pound fresh mushrooms
3 tablespoons butter
3 cups milk
1 cup light cream
½ cup instant dissolving flour
½ cup butter
2 teaspoons finely minced fresh chives
4 teaspoons prepared horseradish, drained
1 teaspoon lemon juice
Salt
Pepper

Cut mushrooms into slices ¼ inch thick and sauté in 3 tablespoons butter until tender. If there is a pool of liquid in pan, continue to cook until liquid evaporates. Set aside. Pour milk and cream into a large saucepan. Stir in flour until flour dissolves. Add ½ cup butter. Cook over a moderate flame, stirring constantly with wire whip, until sauce thickens. Reduce flame and simmer 5 minutes, stirring occasionally. Press horseradish to drain it of bottle liquid. Add shrimp, mushrooms, chives, horseradish, and lemon juice to the sauce. Add salt and pepper to taste. Chill.

❢ Reheat in top section of double boiler or over low flame, stirring frequently.

Dilled Shrimp with Ham and Cucumber

2 pounds (cooked weight) shrimp, boiled, shelled, and deveined
　　(4 pounds raw shrimp)
8 ounces Virginia style baked ham, sliced
2 cups diced cucumber
3 cups medium cream sauce (see page 50)
1 teaspoon dill salt
¾ teaspoon dillweed
1 tablespoon Danish akvavit
Salt
Pepper
½ cup sour cream

Cut ham into ½ inch squares. Peel cucumber and cut lengthwise in half. With teaspoon scrape out and discard seeds. Again cut cucumber in half lengthwise, then cut crosswise into ½ inch slices. Combine cream sauce, shrimp, ham, cucumber, dill salt, dillweed, and ¼ teaspoon pepper. Simmer 3 minutes. Add akvavit. Add salt and pepper if necessary. Chill.

❡ Reheat in top of double boiler or over low flame, stirring frequently. Remove from heat. Stir in sour cream. Do not cook after cream is added or sauce may curdle.

Broiled Shrimp Oreganata

4 pounds raw shrimp in shell
Olive oil
Salt
Pepper
Oregano
3 cups bread crumbs
12 tablespoons (6 ounces) melted butter
1 teaspoon oregano
½ teaspoon leaf thyme
4 cans (8 ounces each) tomato sauce
2 teaspoons anchovy paste
2 tablespoons finely minced parsley
½ cup finely minced roasted sweet red peppers

Peel and devein shrimp. Cut shrimp lengthwise down back without separating into halves. Press shrimp to flatten. Brush shrimp lightly with oil. Sprinkle cut side with salt, pepper, and oregano. In a mixing bowl combine bread crumbs, melted butter, and 1 teaspoon oregano. Rub thyme between fingers to crush it and add to bread crumbs. Mix crumbs well with fork to blend seasoning. Place shrimp, cut side up, in a single layer in shallow casseroles or pans. Sprinkle and pat bread crumbs on shrimp. Chill. In a saucepan combine tomato sauce, anchovy paste, parsley, and sweet peppers, mixing well. Chill.

❡ Preheat oven at 450 degrees. Sprinkle shrimp with oil and bake 5 to 8 minutes. Heat sauce until it boils. Place shrimp under broiler for a minute or two, watching constantly, to brown bread crumbs evenly. Pour sauce over shrimp or pass separately at table.

Broiled Shrimp with Curried Tomato Sauce

4 pounds raw shrimp in shell
Salad oil
Salt
Pepper
Ground cumin
Bread crumbs
¼ pound melted butter
16 ounce can tomatoes
2 tablespoons butter
½ cup very finely minced onions
1 teaspoon very finely minced garlic
4 teaspoons curry powder
16 ounce can tomato puree

Peel and devein shrimp. Cut shrimp lengthwise down back without separating into halves. Press shrimp to flatten. Brush shrimp lightly with oil. Sprinkle cut side with salt, pepper, and cumin. Dip cut side in bread crumbs. Place shrimp, breaded side up, in a single layer in shallow casseroles or pans. Sprinkle melted butter generously on shrimp. Chill. Put tomatoes in blender and blend at high speed ½ minute. Melt 2 tablespoons butter in saucepan. Add onions, garlic, and curry powder. Sauté a minute or two, but do not brown onions. Add tomatoes and tomato puree. Stir well. Simmer over low flame 20 minutes. Season with salt and pepper. Chill.

❡ Preheat broiler flame. Reheat sauce. Place shrimp under broiler for about 3 minutes, or until browned lightly. Do not turn shrimp. Pour sauce over shrimp or serve separately at table.

Coquille of Shrimp with Provolone

NOTE: For extra hearty appetites this recipe may be doubled.

> 8 large-size coquilles (scallop shells)
> 1 pound (cooked weight) shrimp, boiled, shelled, and deveined
>   (2 pounds raw shrimp)
> 2 tablespoons butter
> ¼ pound fresh mushrooms, diced small
> ½ cup onions diced small
> 2 cans (10½ ounces each) condensed cream of potato soup, undiluted
> 1 teaspoon lemon juice
> 2 teaspoons worcestershire sauce
> Salt
> Pepper
> Parmesan cheese, freshly grated
> ½ pound provolone cheese, sliced
> Paprika

Wash and dry 8 large coquille shells. Cut shrimp crosswise into ½ inch slices. Melt butter in saucepan and sauté mushrooms and onions until both are tender. If any mushroom liquid remains in pan, cook until it is evaporated. Combine shrimp, mushrooms, onions, potato soup, lemon juice, and worcestershire sauce. Add salt and pepper to taste. Spoon shrimp mixture into coquille shells. Sprinkle with grated cheese. Cut each slice of provolone into ½ inch strips. Place strips on shrimp mixture. Sprinkle lightly with paprika. Chill.

❡ Preheat oven at 375 degrees. Bake 20 to 25 minutes.

Brochette of Shrimp with Avocado Dip

4 pounds raw shrimp in shell
24 medium-size mushrooms
Salad oil
Salt
Pepper
French dressing
Bread crumbs

Remove shells and veins from shrimp. Sauté mushrooms in 3 tablespoons salad oil until mushrooms are about half done. Sprinkle with salt and pepper. Remove from pan. Dip shrimp in French dressing. Fasten mushrooms and shrimp on skewers, allowing 3 mushrooms to each skewer, one at each end and one in center. Skewer should pierce each shrimp between head and tail. Dip in bread crumbs. Chill.

❦ Preheat broiler. Broil shrimp about 3 minutes on each side. Serve with AVOCADO DIP (recipe follows).

Avocado Dip

1 large soft ripe avocado, peeled and diced (about 2 cups)
1 tablespoon lime juice
2 teaspoons sugar
¼ cup mayonnaise
½ teaspoon worcestershire sauce
6 slices bacon
¼ cup very finely minced onion

Force avocado through a large sieve. Mix with lime juice, sugar, mayonnaise, and worcestershire sauce, blending well. Sauté bacon until very crisp. Remove from pan. Throw off fat, leaving only enough fat in pan to sauté onion. Sauté onion until limp but not brown. Chop bacon fine. Add bacon and onion to avocado mixture. Cover and chill.

Shrimp with Catsup Cream

2 pounds (cooked weight) shrimp, boiled, shelled, and deveined
  (4 pounds raw shrimp)
8 tablespoons butter
¼ cup medium dry sherry
Salt
Celery salt
Pepper
1 cup catsup
2 cups light sweet cream
8 slices toast

❦ This dish may be prepared in the kitchen or at the table with your guests. Just before serving time, prepare toast and cut diagonally. Melt butter in large chafing dish over direct flame, or in large shallow saucepan over trivet and burner. Add shrimp and sherry. When shrimp are coated with butter and warm, sprinkle with salt, celery salt, and pepper. Add catsup, mixing well. Add cream. Stir occasionally and cook until cream bubbles. Spoon shrimp over toast on serving dishes.

Patty of Scallops and Water Chestnuts

8 baked patty shells
2 pounds scallops
1 cup dry white wine
1 cup water
6 tablespoons butter
2 tablespoons finely minced shallots or scallions, white part only
6 tablespoons flour
2 cups hot light cream
2 cans (6 ounces each) water chestnuts, drained and thinly sliced
1 tablespoon very finely minced parsley
Salt
White pepper

If sea scallops are used, cut into ¾ inch cubes. Bay scallops should be left whole. Place scallops in a saucepan with wine, water, and 1 teaspoon salt. Bring to a boil. Reduce flame and simmer 5 minutes. Drain scallops, reserving liquid. Melt butter in another saucepan. Sauté shallots or scallions 1 minute. Stir in flour, blending well. Slowly stir in scallop stock. Slowly add cream. Bring to a boil, reduce flame, and simmer 5 minutes. Remove from fire. Add scallops, water chestnuts, and parsley. Add salt and pepper to taste. Chill.

❡ Preheat oven at 350 degrees. Heat patty shells about 5 minutes. Reheat scallops in double boiler or over very low flame, stirring frequently. Spoon scallops into and alongside patty shells on serving plates.

Scallops Marinara

2 pounds scallops
28 ounce can tomatoes
6 ounce can tomato paste
8 ounce can tomato sauce
2 teaspoons anchovy paste
2 tablespoons olive oil
½ cup finely minced onions
1 teaspoon very finely minced garlic
1 teaspoon basil
½ teaspoon oregano
¼ teaspoon rosemary
Salt
Pepper
Sugar

If sea scallops are used, cut into ¾ inch cubes. Bay scallops should be left whole. Put tomatoes, tomato paste, tomato sauce, and anchovy paste in blender. Blend smooth and set aside. Heat oil in saucepan over low flame. Add onions, garlic, basil, oregano, and rosemary. Sauté until onions are yellow but not brown. Add tomato mixture. Simmer slowly 30 minutes. Place scallops in another saucepan with 2 cups water and ½ teaspoon salt. Bring to a boil. Reduce flame and simmer 5 minutes. Remove scallops from liquid. Cook liquid until it is reduced to 1 cup and add to sauce. Add scallops to sauce. Add salt, pepper, and sugar to taste. Chill.

❡ Reheat scallops in double boiler or over very low flame. Serve with rice or pasta.

Coquille of Lobster and Mushrooms

16 coquilles (scallop shells) about 4 inches from front to back
8 boiled live northern lobsters, about 1¼ pounds each
½ cup butter
1 pound fresh mushrooms, diced small
¼ cup very finely minced onions
½ cup dry white wine
½ cup flour
1 quart hot milk
1 tablespoon Pernod
2 teaspoons lemon juice
Salt
Pepper
1½ cups bread crumbs
6 tablespoons melted butter
1 small onion, grated

Remove meat from lobsters. Cut into small dice no more than ¼ inch thick and set aside. Melt ½ cup butter in a large saucepan. Add mushrooms and minced onions. Sauté until mushrooms are tender. If any mushroom liquid remains in pan, cook until it evaporates. Add wine and simmer until wine is reduced to about 2 tablespoons. Stir in flour, mixing well until no dry flour is visible. Slowly stir in hot milk. Bring to a boil, reduce flame, and simmer 5 minutes, stirring frequently. Remove from fire. Stir in lobster, Pernod, lemon juice, and salt and pepper to taste. Chill mixture in refrigerator. Spoon mixture into coquilles. Combine bread crumbs, melted butter, and grated onion, mixing well. Spread bread crumbs on top of lobster mixture. Chill.

❡ Preheat oven at 375 degrees. Bake 15 minutes. Place coquilles under broiler flame very briefly, watching constantly, to brown bread crumbs.

Coquille of Mussels and Potatoes

16 coquilles (scallop shells) about 4 inches from front to back
4 tins (9 ounces each) mussels in brine
4 slices stale white bread
Milk
½ cup finely minced onions
¼ cup finely minced green pepper
2 tablespoons butter
2 quarts potatoes, peeled and sliced ½ inch thick
4 tablespoons melted butter
Salt
Pepper
4 hard-boiled eggs, chopped fine
1 tablespoon finely minced parsley
1 tablespoon lemon juice
1 cup bread crumbs
4 tablespoons melted butter
Parmesan cheese, freshly grated

Drain mussels. Chop mussels coarsely, discarding juice. Soak bread in milk to cover. Squeeze gently to remove excess milk and chop bread fine. Sauté onions and green pepper in 2 tablespoons butter only until onions are tender. Boil potatoes in salted water until soft. Mash potatoes, adding 4 tablespoons melted butter and salt and pepper to taste. In a mixing bowl combine mussels, bread, onion mixture, hard-boiled eggs, parsley, and lemon juice. Add salt and pepper to taste. Divide mixture among coquilles. Spread mashed potatoes on top. Potatoes may be softened with a small amount of milk or cream to spread evenly. Combine bread crumbs and 4 tablespoons butter. Spread on top of potatoes and sprinkle with cheese. Chill.

❆ Preheat oven at 375 degrees. Bake 15 to 20 minutes. Coquilles may be placed under broiler flame for several minutes to brown topping; watch constantly to avoid scorching.

Oyster Shortcake

6 dozen medium to large size shucked oysters
Milk
½ cup butter
¼ cup finely minced shallots or scallions, white part only
½ cup flour
½ cup heavy cream
1 tablespoon very finely minced dill
1 tablespoon very finely minced parsley
¼ cup very dry sherry
Salt
Celery salt
White pepper

Place oysters together with their own liquor in saucepan and simmer only until oysters curl slightly at edges. Lift oysters out of pan and set aside. Drain juice from pan, measure, and add enough milk to make 1 quart. Heat up to boiling point. Melt butter in another saucepan, add shallots or scallions, and sauté 1 minute. Stir in flour, blending well. Slowly stir in milk mixture, stirring constantly with wire whip. Add cream. Bring to a boil, reduce flame, and simmer 5 minutes. Add dill, parsley, and sherry. Season rather generously with salt, celery salt, and pepper. Add oysters. Chill. Make SWEET PEPPER BISCUITS (recipe follows) and set aside.

❦ Preheat oven at 375 degrees. Heat biscuits in oven 5 minutes. Reheat oysters over low flame or in a double boiler. Split biscuits. Spoon oyster mixture between and over biscuit halves.

Sweet Pepper Biscuits

1½ cups all-purpose flour, sifted before measuring
½ cup cake flour, sifted before measuring
3 teaspoons baking powder
½ teaspoon salt
⅓ cup butter
Milk
1 egg, beaten
¼ cup minced sweet roasted peppers

Preheat oven at 450 degrees. Sift together both kinds of flour, baking powder, and salt. Cut in butter with pastry blender until particles of butter are no larger than rice grains. Add enough milk to egg to make ¾ cup liquid. Add ½ cup of the liquid and peppers to dry ingredients and stir with fork. Add balance of liquid, or as much as necessary to make dough stick together. If dough is too wet to handle, sprinkle lightly with flour. Knead dough lightly about a dozen times on lightly floured board. Roll to ¾ inch thickness. Cut with biscuit cutter. Place biscuits close together on shallow pan and bake 10 to 12 minutes or until lightly browned. Biscuits can be baked from 6 to 12 hours in advance and set aside in pan at room temperature to be reheated.

Stuffed Soft Clams with Bacon

4 cans (24 ounces each) steamed clams in shell
1½ cups sliced celery
¾ cup sliced onions
2 slices stale white sandwich bread
4 tablespoons melted butter
1 tablespoon very finely minced parsley
¼ teaspoon chervil

¼ teaspoon tarragon
Salt
Celery salt
Pepper
Bread crumbs
About 20 slices bacon

Remove clams from juice in can. (Unused juice may be used in clam juice cocktail, as a stock for clam chowder, or served hot as clam broth with a dab of butter or unsweetened whipped cream.) Remove and discard top shells of clams. Carefully tear off necks of clams, letting body of clam remain in shell. Set necks aside. Cover celery and onions with water in a saucepan and simmer until vegetables are tender. Discard water in which vegetables were cooked. Dip bread in clam broth and squeeze gently to remove excess liquid. Put clam necks, celery, onions, and bread through meat grinder, using fine blade. If any of the mixture remains in grinder, remove it and chop very fine with a knife. Turn ground mixture into a bowl. Add melted butter, parsley, chervil, and tarragon. Mix well. Season with salt, celery salt, and pepper to taste. Spread a teaspoon of the mixture on top of each clam, making a smooth mound. Sprinkle clams with bread crumbs. Shake off excess. Panfry bacon until three-quarters done; it should not be crisp. Cut each bacon slice into three pieces. Place a piece on top of each clam. Place clams on cookie sheets. Chill.

❡ Preheat oven at 450 degrees. Bake clams 5 minutes. Place under broiler flame, watching constantly, until bacon is crisp to taste.

Creamed Fresh Salmon Popovers

2 pounds fresh salmon steaks
8 popovers (recipe follows)
2 medium-size onions, sliced
2 medium-size carrots, sliced
2 pieces celery, sliced
1 small bay leaf
1 cup dry white wine
2 cans (3 ounces each) sliced mushrooms
2 cups thick cream sauce (see page 50)
1 tablespoon very finely minced fresh dill
Salt
White pepper

Put onions, carrots, celery, and bay leaf in a large saucepan with 4 cups water and the white wine. Add ½ teaspoon salt. Simmer 10 minutes. Add salmon steaks to pan, cover, and simmer 15 minutes. Lift out salmon with large skimmer or slotted spoon. Drain and reserve salmon stock, and discard vegetables. Drain juice from mushrooms, measure, and add enough salmon stock to make 2 cups liquid. Add liquid to cream sauce. Simmer slowly, stirring frequently, about 5 minutes. Add dill, and season with salt and pepper. With a paring knife remove bones and skin of salmon. Break salmon into fairly large chunks. Add salmon and mushrooms to sauce. Cover and chill.

❡ Reheat popovers (if frozen) in a moderate oven (350 degrees) 5 to 7 minutes. Reheat salmon in double boiler or over low flame. Thin sauce with milk if necessary, and avoid scorching. Cut popovers in half vertically. Spoon salmon mixture between popover halves on serving plates.

Popovers

NOTE: Popovers may be made in custard cups or in a cast-iron popover pan that is divided into 11 sections. The standard 2-egg recipe for popovers falls a trifle short of filling the pan properly. The following recipe makes 9 popovers; multiplied 2½ times it will fill the popover pan twice, or make 22 popovers. Each section of the pan must contain the same amount of batter to make finished popovers of the same size. A 1½ ounce jigger is a good measuring unit for each popover.

    1 cup all-purpose flour, sifted before measuring
    ½ teaspoon salt
    2 eggs, beaten
    1 cup milk
    Salad oil, melted butter, or melted shortening

Preheat oven at 425 degrees. Preheat popover pan in oven 10 minutes. Mix eggs, milk, and 1 tablespoon oil in bowl. Sift flour and salt into bowl. Beat with wire whip or rotary beater until batter is barely smooth. Brush popover pan generously with oil. Pour 3 tablespoons (1½ ounces) batter into each section of pan. Place pan in center of oven. Bake 40 to 45 minutes, or until popovers have risen and are well browned. Popovers may be frozen and just before serving placed for 5 to 7 minutes in an oven preheated at 350 degrees.

Salmon Quenelles with Pimiento and Caper Sauce

2 pounds fresh salmon steak
Salt
Celery salt
Pepper
1 medium-size onion, grated
¼ cup bread crumbs
4 eggs, whites and yolks separated
1 cup sour cream

2 teaspoons lemon juice
3 cups medium cream sauce
  (see page 50)
2 jars (3½ ounces each) pimiento
  strips, drained
2 teaspoons anchovy paste
2 tablespoons medium dry sherry
1 tablespoon very finely minced parsley

If possible, have fish dealer bone salmon, remove skin, and grind salmon fine. If it is ground at home, first cut away skin and bone, and cut fish into 1 inch squares. Examine flesh carefully and pull out any bones before grinding. Grind salmon twice through fine blade of meat grinder. Add 1 teaspoon salt, ¼ teaspoon celery salt, and ¼ teaspoon pepper. Add grated onion, bread crumbs, egg whites, sour cream, and lemon juice. Mix extremely well. Chill in refrigerator, covered, 2 to 3 hours. In a large wide saucepan bring 3 inches salted water to a boil. Drop salmon mixture by heaping tablespoonfuls (about 2 tablespoons each) into boiling water. Do not crowd pan, but do job in several batches if necessary. Quenelles will rise to the top. Cover pan and simmer 5 minutes. Replace water as needed during cooking. Remove quenelles with skimmer or slotted spoon and place in a single layer in shallow, lightly greased casserole. Chill. Beat egg yolks slightly. Add a few tablespoons cream sauce to yolks. Simmer remaining cream sauce, add egg yolks slowly, and simmer 2 minutes longer, stirring constantly. Remove from fire. Stir in pimientos, anchovy paste, sherry, and parsley. Chill.

❡ Preheat oven at 375 degrees. Cover casserole with lid or aluminum foil. Reheat quenelles in oven 15 minutes, or until heated through. Reheat sauce in top of double boiler, stirring frequently. Sauce may be thinned with a little milk or cream if desired. Pour hot sauce over quenelles just before serving.

Peppered Haddock Au Gratin

2 pounds haddock filets
Salt
Pepper
1 lemon
2 cups sweet green peppers cut in ½ inch dice
3 tablespoons butter
1 cup prepared roasted sweet red pepper cut in ½ inch dice
1 cup thinly sliced scallions, white and firm part of greens
2 cups milk
6 tablespoons instant dissolving flour
6 tablespoons butter
Parmesan cheese, freshly grated

Rinse haddock well in cold water. Place in a saucepan and sprinkle with salt and pepper. Add enough cold water barely to cover fish. Add juice of lemon. Bring to a boil, reduce flame, and simmer, covered, 5 minutes. Remove fish from pan with skimmer or slotted spoon. Break fish into flakes. Examine fish carefully and remove any stray bones left in filets. Place fish in mixing bowl. Pour off and reserve 1 cup of fish cooking liquid. Sauté green peppers in 3 tablespoons butter until peppers are tender. Add green peppers, red peppers, and scallions to fish in bowl. Pour milk into a saucepan. Stir in flour, mixing until flour dissolves. Add reserved fish cooking liquid and 6 tablespoons butter. Cook over a moderate flame, stirring constantly, until sauce is thick. Reduce flame and simmer 5 minutes. Pour sauce into bowl containing fish mixture. Stir gently and season to taste with salt and pepper. Spoon into large shallow casserole. Sprinkle generously with parmesan cheese. Chill.

❦ Preheat oven at 375 degrees. Bake 20 to 30 minutes. Place under broiler for a minute or two, watching constantly, to brown cheese.

Sole Collops, Deviled Tomato Sauce, and Cheese

2 pounds filet of gray sole
Salad oil
Salt
Celery salt
Pepper
Bread crumbs
6 tablespoons cider vinegar
6 tablespoons dry white wine
½ cup very finely minced onions
3 cans (8 ounces each) tomato sauce
⅓ cup brown sugar
2 tablespoons prepared mustard
½ pound process swiss cheese
Paprika

Wash filets in cold water and dry with paper toweling. Cut filets in half lengthwise. Cut crosswise into 1 inch pieces. Brush one side of fish lightly with oil. Sprinkle same side of fish with salt, celery salt, and pepper. Dip same side of fish into bread crumbs. Place fish, breaded side up, in a single layer on lightly greased shallow pans or casseroles. Chill. Pour vinegar and wine into a saucepan. Add onions and simmer until liquids are reduced to approximately ¼ cup. Add tomato sauce, sugar, and mustard. Mix well, and simmer 5 minutes. Chill. Shred cheese by forcing it through large holes of metal grater. Chill.

❡ Preheat oven at 500 degrees. Reheat sauce over low flame. Bake fish 5 minutes. Pour sauce over fish. Sprinkle with cheese, and sprinkle lightly with paprika. Place under broiler until cheese browns, watching constantly and turning pan, if necessary, to avoid scorching cheese.

Fried Flounder with Sweet-and-Sour Cucumber Sauce

2 pounds filet of flounder	½ cup sugar
Cornstarch	4 tablespoons cold water
2 tablespoons cold water	2 tablespoons catsup
2 eggs, lightly beaten	Salt
Soy sauce	Pepper
Peanut oil	1 cup thinly sliced cucumbers with peel
2 cups clam juice	⅓ cup thinly sliced scallions, white
½ cup vinegar	and green part

Wash filets and dry with paper toweling. Cut each filet in half lengthwise. Cut crosswise into 1 inch sections. Add ½ cup cornstarch and 2 tablespoons cold water to eggs. Beat to make batter; batter may be somewhat lumpy. Set aside. Brush fish on one side only with soy sauce. Heat peanut oil to a depth of ½ inch in electric skillet preheated at 370 degrees. Dip fish into dry cornstarch, coating lightly, and then dip into batter. Fry until light brown on both sides. Frying will have to be done in several batches, replacing oil as necessary. Place fish in a single layer in lightly greased shallow casseroles or pans. Chill. Pour clam juice into saucepan. Stir in vinegar, sugar, and 1 tablespoon soy sauce. Slowly bring to a boil. Dissolve 2 tablespoons cornstarch in 4 tablespoons cold water. Slowly add to sauce and simmer 2 minutes. Remove from flame. Add catsup. Add salt and pepper if desired. Chill.

❡ Reheat sauce over low flame. Preheat oven at 500 degrees. Place fish in oven just long enough to heat it through, about 5 minutes. Fish may be placed under broiler flame for a few seconds just before serving. Add cucumbers and scallions to sauce just before serving. Pour hot sauce over fish in casserole or serving platter. Serve with rice and hot Chinese mustard.

Peppered Sardines and Eggs

4 cans (3¾ ounces each) boneless and skinless sardines, drained
1 pound sliced bacon
6 hard-boiled eggs
3 medium-size green peppers
11½ ounce jar roasted sweet red peppers, drained
1 medium-size Spanish onion
4 cups medium cream sauce (see page 50)
½ cup light cream
2 teaspoons lemon juice
Salt
Pepper
16 slices white sandwich bread
1 cup bread crumbs
⅓ cup melted butter

Cut bacon slices crosswise into fourths. Chop eggs coarsely. Cut green and red peppers into ½ inch squares. Cut onion into ½ inch dice. Heat bacon in a large pan until crisp. Remove bacon from pan, leaving 2 to 3 tablespoons bacon fat in pan. Add onions and green peppers. Sauté until onions and peppers are tender but not brown. Combine cream sauce bacon, eggs, green peppers and onion, red peppers, and light cream. Stir in lemon juice and salt and pepper to taste. Toast bread under broiler on one side only. Spread untoasted side with pepper and egg mixture. Place sardines on top. Stir melted butter into bread crumbs, blending well. Sprinkle bread crumbs on top of sardines and egg mixture. Place on shallow baking pans or cookie sheets. Chill.

❦ Preheat oven at 375 degrees. Bake 12 to 15 minutes. Place under broiler flame for a minute or two, watching constantly, to brown crumbs.

Toasted Sardines with Egg Sauce

4 cans (3¾ ounces each) boneless and skinless sardines
2 cups sliced onions
3 tablespoons salad oil
2½ cups milk
¼ cup instant dissolving flour
4 tablespoons butter
2 teaspoons prepared mustard
½ teaspoon dry mustard
2 hard-boiled eggs, finely chopped
½ teaspoon worcestershire sauce
Salt
White pepper
16 slices white sandwich bread, toasted
Grated parmesan cheese

To prepare onions, peel and cut in half through stem end. Cut into thinnest possible slices. Break slices apart into strips. Sauté onions in oil, stirring constantly, only until onions are semitender, Chinese style. Set aside. Pour milk into saucepan. Stir in flour until flour is completely dissolved. Add butter. Slowly bring to a boil, stirring frequently, until sauce is thick. Reduce flame and simmer 5 minutes, stirring occasionally. Remove from fire. Combine both kinds of mustard. Stir a little sauce into the mustard and then add mustard to the saucepan. Add eggs, worcestershire sauce, and salt and pepper to taste. Place toast on shallow baking pans or cookie sheets. Place 2 sardines on each piece of toast. Sardines may be split lengthwise if desired. Place onions on sardines. Pour egg sauce over onions, spreading evenly to edge of bread. Sprinkle lightly with cheese. Chill.

❶ Preheat oven at 375 degrees. Bake 15 minutes. Place under broiler, watching constantly, until cheese browns lightly.

Fried Scotch Herring Balls

1 quart sliced potatoes
4 tablespoons butter
2 cans (14 ounces each) Scotch herring in tomato sauce
4 teaspoons cider vinegar
½ cup finely minced onions
½ cup finely minced roasted sweet red peppers
Salt
Pepper
Bread crumbs
Flour
3 eggs, well beaten
Oil for deep fat frying

Boil potatoes in salted water until soft. Drain and mash. Add butter and stir until butter melts. Drain herring. (Sauce in can is not used.) Split herring lengthwise and remove center bone. Cut herring into small dice. Add herring, vinegar, onions, peppers, and ½ cup bread crumbs to potatoes. Mix very well, adding salt and pepper to taste. Shape into balls 1 inch in diameter. Roll balls in flour. Dip in eggs, coating thoroughly. Roll in bread crumbs, coating thoroughly. Chill.

❡ Remove herring balls from refrigerator about an hour before serving time. Preheat oil (at least 4 inches deep) at 370 degrees. Using a wire basket, fry herring balls until medium brown. Drain on absorbent paper. Serve with sauceboats of catsup and tartar sauce.

NOTE: Herring balls may be fried ahead of serving time, placed in a shallow pan, and then reheated in a moderate oven for about 10 to 12 minutes, but they will not be as crisp as when freshly fried.

6

Eggs

SCRAMBLED EGGS, one of the oldest dishes in the history of late-night suppers, are still one of the smartest and simplest. There are times when friends will stay on in your home late at night, and you may want to urge them to stay, even though you had no collation planned. It's a rather pleasant kind of emergency, and the best device for luring them on is a platter of scrambled eggs, which are as well loved now as when great-grandmother made them standing above her elaborate Sheffield chafing dish. When you plan in advance to serve scrambled eggs, the varieties of easy egg garnishes are endless.

Scrambled eggs are still a perfect vehicle for demonstrating your way with a spirit lamp. Some chafing dishes are too small for making scrambled eggs for a party of eight in one batch, although for a smaller number of guests the chafing dish may be perfect. Just as good as a chafing dish, and at times more practical for a party of eight, is a large oval porcelain iron pan or a copper pan set over a trivet with one or two burners beneath. For most people's tastes, scrambled eggs should be soft but not soupy or wet looking and with no large pieces on the platter.

There are other good egg dishes, like poached eggs or eggs mollet, but they become impractical when they must be prepared at the last moment for a party of eight. The traditional French omelette also involves too much hurry and worry to be served to four couples at one time. You could conceivably make two omelettes of four eggs each, but the business of turning, filling, and keeping large omelettes hot yet tender is the kind of ticklish job that permits neither you nor your guests to relax. Happily, there's an alternative. Unlike the conventional omelette, the thick Italian frittata or flat pan omelette is comparatively free of last-minute hurdles. You should be prepared to make them in two large pans of equal size, but the opportunities they afford for creative egg cookery are fascinating.

Although scrambled eggs and frittatas must be cooked at the last minute, the egg accompaniments and flavor tidbits that give them sophisticated interest and that naturally take some preparation time are made well in advance. In preparing raw eggs for mixing, open two eggs at a time into a small dish to make sure there are none with blood spots or with an offensive odor (fortunately a rather rare occurrence these days) before turning them into the mixing bowl. After the eggs are beaten but before they are combined with any other ingredient, they should be strained through a large fine sieve to eliminate any odd pieces of shell or foreign matter. Egg dishes should generally be lightly seasoned with salt and pepper, since guests often use the salt and pepper shaker recklessly when eggs are placed before them. Fresh hot toast for egg dishes is most conveniently made under a preheated broiler rather than in the toaster.

Scrambled Eggs with Anchovies, Peppers, and Onions

16 eggs
3 tablespoons cold water
1 large Spanish onion (about 1 pound)
2 large sweet green peppers
2 large sweet red peppers
2 tablespoons salad oil
Butter
½ teaspoon chervil

½ teaspoon summer savory
1 tablespoon very finely minced
  parsley
2 ounce can flat filets of anchovy
Salt
Pepper
Cayenne pepper
¼ cup heavy sweet cream

Peel onion. Cut in half through stem end. Cut crosswise into thinnest possible slices, using a very sharp French knife for cutting. Cut peppers in half. Remove stem ends, seeds, and inner white membrane. Cut peppers crosswise into thinnest possible slices. Heat oil and 2 tablespoons butter in large wide saucepan. Add onion, peppers, chervil, savory, and parsley. Sauté slowly, stirring frequently but keeping pan covered, until vegetables are tender but not brown. Remove from fire. Drain anchovies and cut each anchovy in half lengthwise. Toss anchovies with onion mixture. Season to taste with salt, pepper, and a dash of cayenne. Chill. Beat eggs with 3 tablespoons cold water, ½ teaspoon salt, and ¼ teaspoon pepper. Chill.

❡ Reheat onion mixture over very low flame or in top of double boiler. Melt 4 tablespoons butter in large buffet skillet or large chafing dish over flame. Beat eggs slightly and pour into skillet. Stir frequently, scraping pan bottom from time to time, until eggs are set to desired doneness. Remove from fire. Stir in heavy cream and 2 tablespoons butter. Pass onion mixture separately at table. Serve with toast.

Scrambled Eggs with Kipper Cream Croutons

16 eggs
3 tablespoons cold water
1 cup light cream
½ cup bread crumbs
1 small onion
12 ounce can kippered herring
Salt
Pepper
8 slices white sandwich bread
Butter
Paprika
¼ cup heavy sweet cream

Mix light cream and bread crumbs. Let mixture stand 1 hour in refrigerator. Grate onion into mixture. Drain herring, chop coarsely, and add to mixture. Add salt and pepper to taste. Toast bread under broiler on one side only. Butter untoasted side of bread. Spread kipper mixture evenly on bread. Sprinkle lightly with paprika. Chill. Beat eggs with 3 tablespoons cold water, ½ teaspoon salt, and ¼ teaspoon pepper. Chill.

❡ Preheat broiler. Melt 3 tablespoons butter. Place kipper croutons on shallow baking pan or cookie sheet. Sprinkle melted butter on croutons. Place under broiler until lightly browned. Cut each crouton diagonally in half and keep warm until served. Melt 4 tablespoons butter in large buffet skillet or large chafing dish over flame. Beat eggs slightly and pour into skillet. Stir frequently, scraping pan bottom from time to time, until eggs are set to desired doneness. Remove from fire. Stir in heavy cream and 2 tablespoons butter. Spoon scrambled eggs over croutons or pass croutons separately at table.

Scrambled Eggs with Scallops Poulette and Pine Nuts

16 eggs
3 tablespoons cold water
3 ounces shelled pine nuts
(pignoli)
1 pound scallops
1 cup cold water
½ cup dry white wine
2 tablespoons very finely minced
shallots or scallions, white part

¼ pound button mushrooms, very
thinly sliced
1 cup thick cream sauce (see page 50)
1 teaspoon very finely minced parsley
1 teaspoon very finely minced chives
Salt
Pepper
Butter
¼ cup heavy sweet cream

Preheat oven at 350 degrees. Place pine nuts in small shallow baking pan and bake 10 to 12 minutes, or until light brown. Stir during baking. Sprinkle with salt. If sea scallops are used, cut into chunks no larger than ½ inch thick. Bay scallops should be left whole. Place scallops in pan with 1 cup water, white wine, and ¼ teaspoon salt. Cover pan and bring to a boil. Simmer 5 minutes. Drain scallops and set aside. Reserve scallop stock. Melt 2 tablespoons butter in another saucepan. Add shallots or scallions and mushrooms. Sauté until mushrooms are tender. Combine scallops, scallop stock, mushrooms, cream sauce, parsley, and chives. Add salt and pepper to taste. Chill. Beat eggs with 3 tablespoons cold water, ½ teaspoon salt, and ¼ teaspoon pepper. Chill.

❡ Heat scallop mixture in top of double boiler over barely simmering water until heated through. Melt 4 tablespoons butter in large buffet skillet or large chafing dish over flame. Beat eggs slightly and pour into skillet. Stir frequently, scraping pan bottom from time to time, until eggs are set to desired doneness. Remove from fire. Stir in heavy cream and 2 tablespoons butter. Sprinkle pine nuts over scallops in serving dish. Pass scallops separately at table. Serve with toast.

Scrambled Eggs with Mussels and Bacon

16 eggs
3 tablespoons cold water
5 pounds mussels
16 slices bacon
Bottled sauce Robert

½ teaspoon salt
¼ teaspoon pepper
Butter
¼ cup heavy cream

Sixty-four mussels will be required for this recipe. Since mussels vary considerably in size and quality, it may be necessary to cook several additional pounds to get this number. Discard any mussels that are open. Remove any sea leaves and beard of mussels. Holding mussels under cold running water, scrub with a stiff vegetable brush. Place mussels in a large pot with 1 cup water. Cover with tight-fitting lid. Steam until mussels are wide open. Discard any that do not open. When mussels are cool enough to handle, remove from shells. Fry bacon until half done; it should not be crisp. Cut each slice in half crosswise. Dip mussels in sauce Robert. Wrap each half slice of bacon around two mussels, and fasten mussels and bacon with toothpicks. Continue in this manner with balance of mussels and bacon. Place in a single layer in a shallow pan. Chill. Beat eggs with 3 tablespoons cold water, salt, and pepper. Chill.

❡ Preheat oven at 450 degrees. Bake mussels until bacon is completely cooked. Remove toothpicks. Keep warm until served. Melt 4 tablespoons butter in large buffet skillet or large chafing dish over flame. Beat eggs slightly and pour into skillet. Stir frequently, scraping pan bottom from time to time, until eggs are set to desired doneness. Remove from fire. Stir in heavy cream and 2 tablespoons butter. Pass mussels with eggs. Serve with toast.

Scrambled Eggs with Creamed Smoked Oysters

16 eggs
3 tablespoons cold water
3 cans (3⅔ ounces each) smoked oysters
1 cup celery cut in ½ inch dice
½ cup onions cut in ½ inch dice
4 tablespoons flour
1½ cups hot milk
½ cup hot light cream
2 tablespoons dry vermouth
Salt
Pepper
Butter
¼ cup heavy sweet cream

Drain oysters. Boil celery in salted water until tender, and drain. Melt 4 table-spoons butter in a saucepan. Sauté onions only until tender. Stir in flour, blending well. Slowly add hot milk and hot light cream. Bring to a boil, stirring constantly. Reduce flame and simmer 5 minutes. Stir in vermouth. Gently fold in oysters and celery. Add salt and pepper to taste. Chill. Beat eggs with 3 tablespoons cold water, ½ teaspoon salt, and ¼ teaspoon pepper. Chill.

❡ Reheat oyster mixture over very low flame or in top of double boiler. Melt 4 tablespoons butter in large buffet skillet or large chafing dish over flame. Beat eggs slightly and pour into skillet. Stir frequently, scraping pan bottom from time to time, until eggs are set to desired doneness. Remove from fire. Stir in heavy cream and 2 tablespoons butter. Pass creamed oysters separately at table. Serve with toast.

Scrambled Eggs with Mushrooms in Sour Cream

16 eggs
3 tablespoons cold water
Butter
1 cup very thinly sliced onions
½ pound mushrooms, very thinly sliced
2 teaspoons paprika
1 teaspoon worcestershire sauce
1 pint sour cream
Salt
Pepper
¼ cup heavy sweet cream

Melt 3 tablespoons butter in saucepan. Sauté onions and mushrooms until tender. If any mushroom liquid remains in pan, cook until it is evaporated. Stir in paprika, mixing well. Remove from fire. Add worcestershire sauce and sour cream, blending very well. Add salt and pepper to taste. Chill. Beat eggs with cold water, ½ teaspoon salt, and ¼ teaspoon pepper. Chill.

❡ Heat mushroom mixture in top of double boiler over barely simmering water. Top section of double boiler should not be in contact with water. Heat until mixture is merely warmed through. Melt 4 tablespoons butter in large buffet skillet or large chafing dish over flame. Beat eggs slightly and pour into skillet. Stir frequently, scraping pan bottom from time to time, until eggs are set to desired doneness. Remove from fire. Stir in 2 tablespoons butter and heavy cream. Pass mushroom mixture separately at table. Serve with toast.

Scrambled Eggs with Mushrooms Madeira

16 eggs
3 tablespoons cold water
Salt
Pepper
Butter
1 pound fresh mushrooms
Juice of ½ lemon
3 tablespoons cognac
1 medium-size onion, sliced
1 medium-size carrot, sliced

1 small bay leaf
¼ teaspoon tarragon
¼ teaspoon chervil
¼ cup flour
3 cups beef consommé
1 tablespoon tomato paste
3 tablespoons Madeira or medium dry sherry
Brown gravy color
¼ cup heavy cream

Cut mushrooms into slices ¼ inch thick. Melt 3 tablespoons butter in wide sauce-pan. Add mushrooms to pan. Sprinkle with salt and pepper and juice of ½ lemon. Sauté until mushrooms are tender and no mushroom liquid remains in pan. Add cognac and set aflame. Set mushrooms aside. In another saucepan melt ¼ cup butter. Add onion, carrot, bay leaf, tarragon, and chervil. Sauté until onion is brown. Stir in flour and sauté until flour is light brown. Add consommé and tomato paste. Bring to a boil. Slowly simmer until liquid is reduced to about 2 cups. Strain gravy. Add Madeira, brown gravy color if desired, and salt and pepper to taste. Combine mushrooms and gravy, and simmer 10 minutes. Chill. Beat eggs with 3 tablespoons cold water, ½ teaspoon salt, and ¼ teaspoon pepper. Chill.

❡ Reheat mushrooms over low flame, stirring occasionally. Melt 4 tablespoons butter in large buffet skillet or large chafing dish over flame. Beat eggs slightly and pour into skillet. Stir frequently, scraping pan bottom from time to time, until eggs are set to desired doneness. Remove from fire. Stir in heavy cream and 2 tablespoons butter. Pass mushrooms at table. Serve with toast.

Scrambled Eggs with Mixed Grill

16 eggs
3 tablespoons cold water
8 large fresh mushrooms
4 large fresh tomatoes
8 small breakfast sausages
16 slices Canadian bacon
Salt
Pepper
Paprika
Sugar
Butter
¼ cup heavy cream

Melt 4 tablespoons butter. Wash mushrooms. Place in a skillet with 2 tablespoons melted butter. Sauté mushrooms only until they lose raw appearance. Sprinkle with salt and pepper, and set aside. Preheat broiler. Remove stem end of tomatoes and cut tomatoes in half horizontally. Brush tomatoes with remainder of melted butter. Sprinkle with salt, pepper, sugar, and paprika. Place under broiler about 5 minutes or until tops of tomatoes just begin to brown. Remove from flame. Broil sausages only until they begin to brown. Broil Canadian bacon only until edges curl. Place mushrooms, tomatoes, sausages, and bacon on shallow baking pan. Chill. Beat eggs with 3 tablespoons cold water, ½ teaspoon salt, and ¼ teaspoon pepper. Chill.

❡ Preheat oven at 450 degrees. Place mixed grill in oven and bake 10 minutes, or until tomatoes are tender and sausages well browned. Place mixed grill on serving platter. Melt 4 tablespoons butter in large buffet skillet or large chafing dish over flame. Beat eggs slightly and pour into skillet. Stir frequently, scraping pan bottom from time to time, until eggs are set to desired doneness. Remove from fire. Stir in heavy cream and 2 tablespoons butter. Serve with toast.

Scrambled Eggs with Sausages and Devil Sauce

16 eggs
3 tablespoons cold water
24 small breakfast sausages
1 medium-size onion, sliced
1 medium-size carrot, sliced
1 medium-size piece celery, sliced
½ small bay leaf
¼ cup flour
2½ cups hot beef consommé

½ cup wine vinegar
1 tablespoon tomato paste
1 teaspoon worcestershire sauce
1 tablespoon bottled sauce diable
Brown gravy color
Salt
Pepper
Butter
¼ cup heavy cream

Melt ¼ cup butter in a saucepan over a low flame. Add onion, carrot, celery, and bay leaf. Sauté until onion is brown. Stir in flour and continue to sauté until flour is light brown. Slowly add consommé. Simmer very slowly 30 minutes. In another pan, cook vinegar until it is reduced to ¼ cup. To the saucepan add vinegar, tomato paste, worcestershire sauce, bottled sauce diable, and brown gravy color if desired. Simmer 5 minutes longer. Strain sauce. Add salt and pepper to taste. Chill. Place sausages in a cold frying pan and cook only until sausages are light brown on two sides. Chill. Beat eggs with 3 tablespoons cold water, ½ teaspoon salt, and ¼ teaspoon pepper. Chill.

◖ Preheat oven at 450 degrees. Bake sausages until well browned. Reheat sauce over moderate flame. Melt 4 tablespoons butter in large buffet skillet or large chafing dish over flame. Beat eggs slightly and pour into skillet. Stir frequently, scraping pan bottom from time to time, until eggs are set to desired doneness. Remove from fire. Stir in heavy cream and 2 tablespoons butter. Place sausages on serving platter and spoon sauce on sausages. Serve with toast.

Scrambled Eggs En Croûte with Smoked Salmon

16 eggs
3 tablespoons cold water
Salt
Pepper
Butter
¼ cup heavy cream
8 large kaiser rolls or large club rolls
½ pound smoked salmon, very thinly sliced
½ cup minced onions
2 jars (2 ounces each) pimiento strips, drained
½ cup heavy cream
½ teaspoon very finely minced garlic
1 cup bread crumbs

Beat eggs with 3 tablespoons cold water, ½ teaspoon salt, and ¼ teaspoon pepper. Melt 4 tablespoons butter in very large skillet. Beat eggs slightly and pour into skillet. Stir frequently, scraping pan bottom from time to time, until eggs are set to desired doneness. Remove from fire. Stir in ¼ cup heavy cream and 2 tablespoons butter. Set aside. Cut a thin cap off the top of each roll about ¼ inch from the top. Scrape out soft insides of rolls. (Caps and scraped roll pieces may be made into bread crumbs in blender if desired.) Cut salmon into thinnest possible strips, about 1 inch long. Combine eggs, minced onions, salmon, pimientos, and ½ cup heavy cream. Correct seasoning to taste. Spread insides of rolls with butter, softened if desired. Fill with scrambled egg mixture, forming a mound of egg on top of each roll. Melt ¼ cup butter in a saucepan over very low flame. Add garlic and sauté about 10 seconds. Remove from flame. Stir in bread crumbs, mixing well. Sprinkle over eggs, patting crumbs carefully on egg mounds. Place on cookie sheet. Chill.

❡ Preheat oven at 375 degrees. Place baking pan in oven and bake 15 to 18 minutes.

Scrambled Eggs En Croûte with Ham and Chives

16 eggs
3 tablespoons cold water
Salt
Pepper
Butter
¼ cup heavy cream
8 large kaiser rolls or large club rolls
4 ounces boiled ham, thinly sliced
2 tablespoons very finely minced chives
½ cup heavy cream
½ pound gruyère cheese, shredded
Paprika

Beat eggs with 3 tablespoons cold water, ½ teaspoon salt, and ¼ teaspoon pepper. Melt 4 tablespoons butter in large skillet. Beat eggs slightly and pour into skillet. Stir frequently, scraping pan bottom from time to time, until eggs are set to desired doneness. Remove from fire. Stir in ¼ cup heavy cream and 2 tablespoons butter. Set aside. Cut a thin cap off the top of each roll about ¼ inch from top. Scrape out soft insides of rolls. (Caps and scraped roll pieces may be made into bread crumbs in blender if desired.) Cut ham into tiny dice of about $\frac{1}{16}$ inch. Combine eggs, ham, chives, and ½ cup heavy cream. Mix well. Correct seasoning if desired. Spread insides of rolls with butter, softened if desired. Fill with scrambled egg mixture. Sprinkle shredded gruyère cheese on top. Sprinkle with paprika. Place on shallow baking pan or cookie sheet. Chill.

❑ Preheat oven at 375 degrees. Place baking pan in oven and bake 15 to 18 minutes.

Scrambled Eggs Hero with Mortadella

16 eggs
3 tablespoons cold water
Salt
Pepper
Butter
¼ cup heavy cream
8 hero buns
4 ounces mortadella sausage, thinly sliced
½ teaspoon oregano
1 tablespoon very finely minced parsley
½ cup heavy cream
½ pound provolone cheese, shredded
Paprika

Beat eggs with 3 tablespoons cold water, ½ teaspoon salt, and ¼ teaspoon pepper. Melt 4 tablespoons butter in a very large skillet. Beat eggs slightly and pour into skillet. Stir frequently, scraping pan bottom from time to time, until eggs are set to desired doneness. Remove from fire. Stir in ¼ cup heavy cream and 2 tablespoons butter. Set aside. Cut a thin cap off the top of each hero bun about ¼ inch from the top. Scrape out soft insides of buns. (Caps and scraped bun pieces may be made into bread crumbs in blender if desired.) Cut mortadella into tiny dice of about $\frac{1}{16}$ inch. Combine eggs, mortadella, oregano, parsley, and ½ cup heavy cream. Mix well. Correct seasoning if desired. Spread insides of buns with butter, softened if desired. Fill with scrambled egg mixture. Sprinkle shredded provolone cheese on top and sprinkle with paprika. Place on shallow baking pan or cookie sheet. Chill.

❡ Preheat oven at 375 degrees. Place baking pan in oven and bake 15 to 18 minutes.

Scrambled Eggs En Brioche with Liver Pâté

16 eggs
3 tablespoons cold water
Salt
Pepper
Butter
¼ cup heavy cream
8 large brioches
4 cans (2¾ ounces each) liver pâté, with truffles if possible
½ cup heavy cream
1 cup bread crumbs
1 small onion, grated
1 tablespoon grated parmesan cheese

Beat eggs with 3 tablespoons cold water, ½ teaspoon salt, and ¼ teaspoon pepper. Melt 4 tablespoons butter in large skillet. Beat eggs slightly and pour into skillet. Stir frequently, scraping pan bottom from time to time, until eggs are set to desired doneness. Remove from fire. Stir in ¼ cup heavy cream and 2 tablespoons butter. Set aside. Cut cap off each brioche just below wide section of brioche. Brush inside of cap with butter, softened if desired. Set caps aside. Scrape out insides of brioches leaving a shell about ½ inch thick. (Scraped brioche pieces may be made into bread crumbs in blender if desired.) Spread inside of each brioche with liver pâté. Stir remaining ½ cup heavy cream into eggs. Pile scrambled egg mixture into each brioche, carefully forming a mound of egg on top. Melt ¼ cup butter and mix with bread crumbs, grated onion, and parmesan cheese. Sprinkle over eggs, patting crumbs carefully on egg mounds. Chill stuffed brioches and caps, keeping both covered with clear plastic wrap.

❡ Preheat oven at 375 degrees. Place brioches and caps, buttered side up, in oven and bake 12 to 15 minutes. Place brioche caps on top of eggs on serving platter.

Patty of Hard-boiled Eggs and Finnan Haddie

8 baked patty shells
12 eggs
1 pound finnan haddie
1 cup celery cut in ¼ inch dice
½ cup butter or margarine
½ cup onions cut in ¼ inch dice
½ cup flour
1 quart hot milk
1 cup light cream
2 jars (2 ounces each) pimiento strips, drained
Salt
Pepper
Cayenne pepper
1 tablespoon finely minced parsley

Boil eggs 15 to 20 minutes. Place in cold water for ½ hour. Remove shells and set aside. Wash finnan haddie. Place in saucepan with cold water to cover. Simmer, covered, about ½ hour or until fish flakes easily. Remove bones and skin. Break fish into flakes and set aside. Boil celery in slightly salted water until tender. Drain and set aside. Melt butter or margarine in a large saucepan. Add onions and sauté only until onions are limp. Stir in flour, blending well. Slowly stir in hot milk. Bring to a boil. Reduce flame and simmer 5 minutes, stirring frequently. Cut hard-boiled eggs into large dice. Add eggs, finnan haddie, celery, light cream, and pimientos to sauce. Simmer 5 minutes. Add salt and pepper to taste and a dash of cayenne. Chill.

❡ Preheat oven at 375 degrees. Place brioches and caps, buttered side up, in oven thick it may be thinned with milk or cream. Correct seasoning if necessary. Preheat oven at 350 degrees. Warm patty shells about 5 minutes in oven. Spoon egg mixture into and over patty shells. Sprinkle with chopped parsley.

Frittata with Tomato, Eggplant, and Bacon

12 eggs
3 medium-size ripe tomatoes
1 cup diced eggplant
¼ pound sliced bacon
½ cup finely minced onions
1 teaspoon very finely minced garlic
½ teaspoon basil

¼ teaspoon marjoram
Salad oil
Salt
Pepper
Butter
2 tablespoons cold water

Dip tomatoes in boiling water for 20 seconds. Peel tomatoes and cut off stem ends. Cut tomatoes into quarters, squeeze out seeds, and chop coarsely. Drain well and set aside. Peel eggplant. Cut into ¼ inch slices, then cut into ¼ inch dice. Place eggplant in a pan with 2 tablespoons oil and 1 cup water. Boil, covered, till tender. Drain well. Panfry the bacon till crisp. Drain. Chop bacon coarsely. In another pan melt 1 tablespoon butter. Sauté the onions, garlic, basil, and marjoram until onions are merely soft, not colored. Beat eggs with 2 tablespoons cold water. Stir in tomatoes, eggplant, bacon, onion mixture, ½ teaspoon salt, ¼ teaspoon pepper. Chill.

❡ Preheat broiler. Brush 2 heavy skillets (10 inches across top) lightly on bottoms and sides with a thin film of oil. Add 2 tablespoons butter to each skillet. Place over a moderate flame. Beat eggs slightly. When butter begins to sputter, add half the egg mixture to each pan. As eggs begin to set, lift eggs to let uncooked part flow to bottom of pan. When tops show signs of becoming firm, place frittatas under broiler until tops are firm. Slide spatula under each frittata to make sure it will come loose easily. Invert frittatas onto serving plates. Cut into wedges at table.

Frittata with Chicken Livers and Noodles

12 eggs
1 cup fine-size noodles
½ pound chicken livers
¼ pound fresh mushrooms
½ cup finely minced onions
1 teaspoon very finely minced garlic
¼ teaspoon thyme
Salt
Pepper
Salad oil
Butter
2 tablespoons cold water

Break noodles into small pieces. Boil in salted water until tender. Drain. Cut chicken livers in half. Heat 1 tablespoon oil in saucepan with 1 tablespoon butter. Add livers, sprinkle with salt and pepper, and sauté until livers are browned; they should be a little pink inside. When livers are cool enough to handle, cut into ¼ inch slices. Set aside. Cut mushrooms into ¼ inch dice. In a clean saucepan melt 2 tablespoons butter. Sauté mushrooms, onions, garlic, and thyme until onions and mushrooms are tender and no mushroom liquid remains in pan. Beat eggs with 2 tablespoons cold water. Stir in chicken livers, noodles, mushroom mixture, ½ teaspoon salt, and ¼ teaspoon pepper. Chill.

❡ Preheat broiler. Brush 2 heavy skillets (10 inches across top) lightly on bottoms and sides with a thin film of oil. Add 2 tablespoons butter to each skillet. Place over a moderate flame. Beat eggs slightly. When butter begins to sputter, add half the egg mixture to each pan. As eggs begin to set, lift eggs to let uncooked portion flow to bottom of pan. When tops show signs of becoming firm, place frittatas under broiler till tops are firm. Slide spatula under each frittata to make sure it will come loose easily. Invert frittatas onto large serving plates. Cut into wedges at table.

Frittata with Lobster and Asparagus

12 eggs
¾ pound frozen small rock lobster tails
1 pound fresh asparagus
¼ cup fresh mushrooms
½ cup finely minced onions
2 tablespoons freshly grated parmesan cheese
Butter
Salt
Pepper
2 tablespoons cold water
Salad oil

Cook lobster tails following directions on package. Remove lobster meat from shells and cut into thin slices. Peel asparagus with vegetable peeler. Cut off hard bottoms of stems. Cook asparagus in slightly salted water until just tender. Drain. Cut asparagus crosswise into ½ inch pieces. Cut mushrooms into ¼ inch dice. Melt 2 tablespoons butter in saucepan. Sauté mushrooms and onions together, stirring frequently until both are tender and no mushroom liquid remains in pan. Beat eggs with 2 tablespoons cold water. Stir in lobster, asparagus, mushroom mixture, parmesan cheese, ½ teaspoon salt, and ¼ teaspoon pepper. Chill.

❡ Preheat broiler. Brush 2 heavy skillets (10 inches across top) lightly on bottoms and sides with a thin film of oil. Add 2 tablespoons butter to each skillet. Place over a moderate flame. Beat eggs slightly. When butter begins to sputter, add half the egg mixture to each pan. As eggs begin to set, lift eggs to let uncooked portion flow to bottom of pan. When tops show signs of becoming firm, place frittatas under broiler till tops are firm. Slide spatula under each frittata to make sure it will come loose easily. Invert frittatas onto large serving plates. Cut into wedges at table.

Frittata with Italian Sweet and Hot Sausages

12 eggs
1 pound Italian sweet sausages
¼ pound Italian hot sausages
1 cup diced green peppers
3 medium-size ripe tomatoes
1 cup boiled diced potatoes
2 teaspoons finely minced parsley
Butter
Salt
Pepper
2 tablespoons cold water
Salad oil

Cut peppers into ¼ inch dice. Heat 2 tablespoons butter in a skillet and sauté peppers until tender. Set aside. Dip tomatoes into boiling water for 20 seconds. Peel tomatoes and cut off stem ends. Cut tomatoes into quarters, squeeze out seeds, and chop coarsely. Drain well. Set aside. Cut potatoes into ¼ inch dice. Preheat oven at 400 degrees. Place sausages in a shallow pan. Pierce sausages with a kitchen fork. Bake 20 to 30 minutes or until well browned. Drain sausages and cut into ¼ inch slices. Beat eggs with 2 tablespoons cold water. Stir in sausages, peppers, tomatoes, potatoes, parsley, ½ teaspoon salt, and ¼ teaspoon pepper. Chill.

❡ Preheat broiler. Brush 2 heavy skillets (10 inches across top) lightly on bottoms and sides with a thin film of oil. Add 2 tablespoons butter to each skillet. Place over a moderate flame. Beat eggs slightly. When butter begins to sputter, add half the egg mixture to each pan. As eggs begin to set, lift eggs to let uncooked part flow to bottom of pan. When tops show signs of becoming firm, place frittatas under broiler until tops are firm. Slide spatula under each frittata to make sure it will come loose easily. Invert frittatas onto serving plates. Cut into wedges at table.

Frittata with Ham, Artichoke Hearts, and Pepper

12 eggs
6 ounce jar artichoke hearts marinated in oil, well drained
½ pound boiled ham, thinly sliced
7½ ounce jar roasted peppers, drained
½ cup very finely minced onions
1 teaspoon very finely minced garlic
2 teaspoons very finely minced parsley
Butter
Salt
Pepper
2 tablespoons cold water
Salad oil

Cut artichoke hearts in half, then cut into ¼ inch dice. Cut ham and peppers into ¼ inch dice. Melt 2 tablespoons butter in a small saucepan. Sauté onions and garlic only until onions are soft, not colored. Beat eggs with 2 tablespoons cold water. Stir in artichoke hearts, ham, peppers, onion mixture, parsley, ½ teaspoon salt, and ¼ teaspoon pepper. Chill.

❡ Preheat broiler. Brush 2 heavy skillets (10 inches across top) lightly on bottoms and sides with a thin film of oil. Add 2 tablespoons butter to each skillet. Place over a moderate flame. Beat eggs slightly. When butter begins to sputter, add half the egg mixture to each pan. As eggs begin to set, lift eggs to let uncooked portion flow to bottom of pan. When tops of frittatas show signs of becoming firm, place frittatas under broiler until tops are firm. Slide spatula under each frittata to make sure it will come loose from pan easily. Invert frittatas onto serving plates or platters. Cut into wedges at table.

Frittata with Genoa Salami and Potatoes

12 eggs
6 ounces genoa salami, very thinly sliced
1 cup bread croutons
2 medium-size potatoes, boiled
½ cup finely minced onions
1 teaspoon very finely minced garlic
¼ teaspoon oregano
Butter
Salt
Pepper
2 tablespoons cold water
Salad oil

Cut enough narrow white Italian bread into ¼ inch cubes to make cup of croutons. Sprinkle with 2 tablespoons oil (olive oil preferred), place in shallow pan, and bake in preheated oven at 375 degrees until brown, 10 to 12 minutes. Chill. Cut salami into ¼ inch squares. Cut potatoes into ¼ inch cubes. Melt 2 tablespoons butter in saucepan. Sauté onions, garlic, and oregano until onions are tender but not colored. Beat eggs with 2 tablespoons cold water. Stir in salami, potatoes, onion mixture, ½ teaspoon salt, and ¼ teaspoon pepper. Chill.

❡ Preheat broiler. Brush 2 heavy skillets (10 inches across top) lightly on bottoms and sides with a thin film of oil. Stir bread croutons into egg mixture and beat slightly. Add 2 tablespoons butter to each skillet. Place over a moderate flame. When butter begins to sputter, add half the egg mixture to each pan. As eggs begin to set, lift eggs to let uncooked part flow to bottom of pan. When tops of frittatas show signs of becoming firm, place frittatas under broiler until tops are firm. Slide spatula under each frittata to make sure it will come loose from pan easily. Invert frittatas onto serving plates or platters. Cut into wedges at table.

7

Meat and Poultry

IN THIS COUNTRY a midnight collation of meat or poultry follows a custom becoming ever more happily and sensibly accepted—a portion of meat or poultry late at night will be one that's light but satisfying, never one of those Diamond Jim Brady spreads that used to leave guests groggy in their chairs. For suppers during the later hours of the night, chicken and beef lead the parade, with veal, lamb, and pork showing up less frequently. The one-pound steak normally eaten in a steak house at the dinner hour is properly reduced to a trimmed, fat-free minute steak of six or eight ounces. For a large group of people at a late-night feast, three-to-four-inch shell steaks are sometimes broiled only to be sliced thin and served in small portions nestling in hamburger buns. In creating interesting chicken dishes the possibilities for fowl play, one might say, are infinite, since the naturally light flavor of chicken lends itself to so many flights of the cook's fancy.

When you buy beef for steaks or for dishes like the thinly sliced Chinese beef and mushrooms, beef with some age is best. Avoid the kind of beef—found especially in supermarkets—whose telltale moist redness indicates the beef was slaughtered one day and on the meat counter the next, thus permitting the dealer to avoid shrinkage that occurs when meat is aged. Even if the beef is the very top grade of U.S. Prime, it needs age for tenderness and flavor development. A reliable meat dealer will advise you if his meat is aged; the tenderness of his meat will usually confirm what he says.

Completely boned and skinless breasts of chicken, called chicken cutlets or filets, are now available in many markets. In this case, unlike beef for steaks, absolute freshness is the guideline to top quality. Select chicken breasts from a busy meat counter where the stock moves fast. If the boned and skinned breasts are not available, some butchers will do the boning job for you. If you bone the chicken yourself, it pays to invest in a butcher's boning knife and to keep it razor sharp. In dishes calling for cooked chicken, the directions usually specify boiled chicken. The temptation to use leftover roast chicken or turkey is great, but remember that any leftover roast tends to become drier and drier as it stands in the refrigerator. As a substitute for boiled chicken, prepared chicken roll, turkey roll, or breast of turkey that is steamed rather than dry roasted may be used.

Minute Steaks with Onion and Red Wine Sauce

8 tenderloin (filet mignon) steaks or boneless shell steaks,
   6 to 8 ounces each
1 cup very thinly sliced onions
½ cup very thinly sliced mushrooms
Butter
1 cup dry red wine
3 tablespoons flour
2 cups hot beef or chicken stock

1 teaspoon meat extract
⅛ teaspoon dried tarragon
2 teaspoons worcestershire sauce
Salt
Pepper
8 large slices toast
1 bunch watercress

Cut onions in half through stem end. Cut crosswise into thinnest possible slices. Break slices apart to make strips. Separate mushroom caps and stems; cut into strips as thin as onions. Melt 1 tablespoon butter in a saucepan. Add onions and mushrooms. Simmer until onions are yellow but not brown. Add wine. Cook until wine is reduced to about ¼ cup. Set aside. In another saucepan melt 3 tablespoons butter over a low flame. Stir in flour, blending well. Continue to cook, stirring occasionally, for 5 minutes. Slowly stir in beef or chicken stock, meat extract, and tarragon. Mix well. Add onion mixture and simmer ½ hour over low flame. Add worcestershire sauce and salt and pepper to taste.

❡ Reheat sauce over a low flame. Preheat electric griddle or skillet at 400 degrees. Panbroil steaks until done to taste. Sprinkle with salt and pepper. On each serving dish or on platter place a steak on a slice of toast. Pour sauce on steaks or pass separately at table. Garnish steaks with watercress.

Minute Steaks with Stuffed Artichoke Bottoms

8 tenderloin (filet mignon) steaks or
  boneless shell steaks, 6 to 8
  ounces each
2 cans (12 ounces each) artichoke
  bottoms
8 slices stale white bread
Butter
⅓ cup finely minced green peppers
⅓ cup finely minced onions
2 eggs, beaten

1 tablespoon very finely minced
  parsley
1 tablespoon small capers in vinegar,
  drained
Salt
Pepper
Prepared toasted bread crumbs
8 large slices toast
½ lemon

Drain artichoke bottoms and wash under cold running water. Sixteen artichoke bottoms will be needed. (There may be a few extra, which can be used in salads.) Dry on paper toweling. If bread is thin use 12 slices. Bread is best if three or four days old but not completely hard. Cut crust off bread. Cut bread into large dice. Place in blender in small batches and blend at high speed until crumbs are formed. Set aside. Melt 6 tablespoons butter in a saucepan. Add green peppers and onions. Sauté until vegetables are tender but not brown. Remove from flame. In a mixing bowl combine bread crumbs, sautéed vegetables, eggs, parsley, and capers. Add salt and pepper to taste. Fill each artichoke bottom with smooth mound of stuffing. Sprinkle with prepared toasted crumbs. Melt 3 tablespoons butter and dab top of stuffing with melted butter. Place artichoke bottoms on a greased shallow pan. Chill.

❦ Preheat oven at 375 degrees. Bake artichoke bottoms 20 minutes or until browned. Preheat electric griddle or skillet at 400 degrees. Panbroil steaks until done to taste. Sprinkle with salt and pepper. On each serving dish or platter place a steak on a slice of toast. Brush with butter. Sprinkle with a few drops of lemon juice. Place 2 artichoke bottoms alongside each steak.

Minute Steaks, Eggplant, and Pimiento Au Gratin

8 tenderloin (filet mignon) steaks or boneless shell steaks,
  6 to 8 ounces each
8 slices of large eggplant ¾ inch thick
2 eggs
¼ cup milk
Flour
Salad oil
8 slices provolone cheese
2 cups medium cream sauce (see page 50)
2 jars (2 ounces each) sliced pimientos, drained
Grated parmesan cheese
Salt
Pepper
Butter
½ lemon

Peel eggplant. (If eggplant is small or narrow, use 2 slices per portion.) Beat eggs and milk. Dip eggplant in flour and then dip in egg mixture. Prepare more egg-milk mixture if necessary. Heat ¼ inch oil in a large skillet. Sauté eggplant until medium brown on both sides or until tender when tested with two-pronged fork. Place eggplant in a single layer on a greased shallow baking pan. Place provolone cheese on eggplant, cutting cheese if necessary to fit eggplant slices. Spoon cream sauce on cheese. Sprinkle with pimientos. Sprinkle with parmesan cheese. Chill.

❧ Preheat oven at 400 degrees. Preheat electric griddle or skillet at 400 degrees. Bake eggplant in oven 20 minutes. Panbroil steaks until done to taste. Sprinkle with salt and pepper. Brush steaks with butter. Squeeze a few drops lemon juice on top. Place a portion of eggplant alongside each steak on serving platter or plates.

Minute Steaks with Deviled Hollandaise and Baked Tomatoes

8 tenderloin (filet mignon) steaks or boneless shell steaks,
   6 to 8 ounces each
6 egg yolks
6 ounces melted butter
1 tablespoon lemon juice
Salt
Pepper
Cayenne pepper
4 large tomatoes
4 tablespoons soft butter or margarine
Brown sugar
1 tablespoon bottled sauce diable
1 teaspoon Dijon mustard
½ teaspoon dry mustard

Sauce should be prepared about an hour or two before party time. Place egg yolks in blender. Melt 6 ounces butter over low flame until very hot but not bubbling. Run blender at low speed and keep butter on very low flame. Add butter to blender in very small quantities, no more than a tablespoon at a time. Continue adding hot butter until it is all used. Season with lemon juice, salt, pepper, and a generous dash of cayenne. Keep sauce covered in a warm place until served. It should not be placed over a flame or a double boiler. Cut out stem ends of tomatoes. Cut tomatoes in half. Spread cut sides with soft butter or margarine. Sprinkle with salt and pepper. Sprinkle with brown sugar. Place tomatoes on a greased shallow pan. Chill.

❡ Preheat oven at 450 degrees. Bake tomatoes 10 to 15 minutes or until tender. Stir sauce diable and both kinds of mustard to a smooth paste. Stir into hollandaise sauce. Preheat electric griddle or skillet at 400 degrees. Panbroil steaks until done to taste. Sprinkle with salt and pepper. Spoon sauce on steaks. Place a baked tomato alongside each steak on serving plates or platter.

Minute Steaks with Mushrooms Stroganoff

8 tenderloin (filet mignon) steaks or
    boneless shell steaks, 6 to 8 ounces each
1½ teaspoons caraway seeds
1 pound fresh mushrooms
2 tablespoons salad oil
2 tablespoons lemon juice
Salt

Pepper
Butter
½ cup onions cut in small dice
4 tablespoons flour
2 cups hot beef or chicken stock
1 cup sour cream
8 large slices toast

Pound caraway seeds in a small mortar until caraway aroma is very pronounced. Set aside. Separate mushroom caps and stems. Cut caps into slices ⅛ inch thick. Cut mushroom stems lengthwise into slices ⅛ inch thick. Heat oil in a large skillet. Add mushrooms. Sprinkle with lemon juice and salt and pepper. Sauté mushrooms until done and all mushroom liquid has evaporated from pan. In a saucepan over a low flame melt 4 tablespoons butter. Add onions and sauté until onions are yellow but not brown. Stir in flour. Stir in beef or chicken stock in small batches, stirring well after each addition. Add caraway seeds. Bring sauce to a boil. Reduce flame and simmer 5 minutes, stirring frequently. Combine sauce and mushrooms in one pan and simmer 5 minutes. Add salt and pepper to taste. Let mixture chill slightly. Stir in sour cream. Correct seasoning if necessary. Chill.

❦ Reheat mushrooms in top part of double boiler over simmering water. Preheat electric griddle or skillet at 400 degrees. Panbroil steaks until done to taste. Sprinkle with salt and pepper. Brush with butter. On each serving dish or platter place a steak on a slice of toast. Spoon mushrooms alongside steak.

Skewered Chili Steaks

4 pounds boneless sirloin steak
4 large cloves garlic
½ cup salad oil
1 tablespoon chili powder
1 teaspoon ground cumin
2 tablespoons cider vinegar
2 cups sliced onions
Salt
Pepper
½ cup catsup
½ cup mayonnaise
2 teaspoons chili powder
¼ teaspoon Tabasco sauce
1 tablespoon lemon juice
1 tablespoon sugar

Cut steak into 1 inch squares about ¼ inch thick. Cut cloves of garlic in half. In a mixing bowl combine salad oil, 1 tablespoon chili powder, cumin, vinegar, onions, and garlic. Add meat. Season generously with salt and pepper. Toss ingredients well. Let mixture marinate in refrigerator 3 to 4 hours. In a small mixing bowl combine catsup, mayonnaise, 2 teaspoons chili powder, Tabasco sauce, lemon juice, and sugar. Chill. Remove meat from marinade. Fasten meat on 8 skewers. Chill.

❈ Preheat broiler flame or prepare charcoal fire. Broil skewered steaks until medium brown on two sides. Serve with cold chili dip.

Chinese Beef and Mushrooms with Oyster Sauce

3 pounds sirloin steak 1½ inches
   thick
Salt
Pepper
4 egg whites, beaten
½ cup cornstarch
1 teaspoon M.S.G. seasoning
Peanut oil
1 pound fresh button mushrooms

¼ cup very finely minced onion
½ teaspoon very finely minced
   garlic
½ teaspoon very finely minced
   fresh ginger
2 cups chicken broth or stock
2 tablespoons Chinese oyster sauce
2 tablespoons cornstarch
1 teaspoon sugar

Cut away all bone, fat, gristle, and seams from meat. Cut across grain into 1½ inch squares as thin as possible. Sprinkle with salt and pepper. Mix egg whites, ½ cup cornstarch, and M.S.G. seasoning until very smooth. Add meat to egg mixture, stirring well. Heat 4 tablespoons oil in large skillet or wok. Add meat to pan piece by piece and sauté in small batches until meat is brown on both sides. Replace oil in pan if necessary while sautéing meat. Place beef in mixing bowl. Clean skillet and sauté mushrooms in 3 tablespoons oil until done. Set aside. In a saucepan heat 2 tablespoons oil over low flame. Add onion and garlic. Sauté 1 minute. Add ginger, chicken broth or stock, and oyster sauce, stirring well. Dissolve 2 tablespoons cornstarch in 4 tablespoons cold water. When chicken broth boils, slowly stir in cornstarch. Add sugar. Simmer 2 minutes. Add mushrooms and sauce to beef. Chill.

❡ Reheat over a moderate flame until piping hot. Serve with rice or prepared fried noodles, or both, and hot Chinese mustard.

Chinese Beef with Spiced Onions and Cucumber

3 pounds sirloin steak 1½ inches thick
2 eggs, beaten
½ cup cornstarch
2 tablespoons soy sauce
1 tablespoon dry sherry
4 cups thinly sliced onions
2 cups thinly sliced cucumbers

1 tablespoon ground coriander
2 teaspoons ground cumin
¼ cup brown sugar
2 teaspoons soy sauce
2 tablespoons lemon juice
Freshly ground black pepper
Peanut oil

Cut away all bone, fat, gristle, and seams from meat. Cut meat across grain as thin as possible into 1½ inch squares. Mix eggs, cornstarch, 2 tablespoons soy sauce, and sherry until very smooth. Add meat to egg mixture, stirring well. Let meat marinate 20 minutes. Cut onions in half through stem end. Cut crosswise into thinnest possible slices. Peel cucumbers and cut lengthwise in half. Remove seeds with teaspoon. Cut cucumbers crosswise into thinnest possible slices. In a mixing bowl combine onions, cucumbers, coriander, cumin, brown sugar, 2 teaspoons soy sauce, and lemon juice. Sprinkle generously with pepper. Chill. Heat 3 tablespoons oil in large skillet or wok. Add meat to pan piece by piece and sauté in small batches until meat is brown on both sides. Replace oil in pan if necessary while sautéing meat. Chill.

❡ Remove meat and vegetables from refrigerator about ½ hour before serving time. Heat 3 tablespoons oil in a large skillet or wok. Drain vegetables. Stir-fry, stirring constantly, until semitender. Add beef. Continue to stir-fry until beef is hot. Serve with rice or prepared fried noodles, or both, and hot Chinese mustard.

Hamburger with Sesame Onions

2½ pounds chopped top sirloin or top round
3 tablespoons cold water
Salt
Pepper
¼ pound melted butter
2 medium-size Spanish onions
Salad oil
1 tablespoon sesame seeds
2 teaspoons soy sauce
Sugar

Dissolve 2½ teaspoons salt in cold water. Add ½ teaspoon pepper. Pour over meat in mixing bowl. Add melted butter. Toss lightly to blend ingredients. Shape into 8 round or oval hamburgers ¾ inch thick. Chill. Cut onions in half through stem end. Cut crosswise into thinnest possible slices. Break slices apart to make strips. Heat 3 tablespoons oil in large skillet. Add onions. Sauté, stirring frequently, only until onions are half done, Chinese style. Remove from fire. Heat sesame seeds in heavy dry frying pan over moderate flame, stirring constantly, until sesame seeds are medium brown. Avoid scorching. Add sesame seeds to onions. Add soy sauce and salt, pepper, and sugar to taste. Chill.

❡ Preheat electric skillet or griddle at 300 degrees. Brush lightly with oil. Sauté hamburgers until medium brown on both sides. Place onions in a lightly greased skillet and sauté only until heated through. Spoon onions over hamburgers on serving platter or pass separately at table.

Hamburger with Spiced Peppers

2½ pounds chopped top sirloin or
   top round
3 tablespoons cold water
Salt
Pepper
¼ pound melted butter
2 sweet green peppers, about 6
   ounces each
2 sweet red peppers, about 6
   ounces each

1 cup onions sliced very thin
Peanut oil
1 teaspoon very finely minced
   garlic
½ teaspoon very finely minced
   fresh ginger
4 teaspoons soy sauce
¼ teaspoon ground nutmeg
¼ teaspoon ground cloves
Sugar

Dissolve 2½ teaspoons salt in cold water. Add ½ teaspoon pepper. Pour over meat in mixing bowl. Add melted butter. Toss lightly to blend ingredients. Shape into 8 round or oval hamburgers ¾ inch thick. Chill. Cut peppers in half through stem end. Remove stems, seeds, and inner membranes. Cut crosswise into thinnest possible slices. Cut onions in half through stem end. Cut crosswise into thinnest possible slices. Break slices apart to make strips. Heat 4 tablespoons peanut oil in large skillet or wok. Add peppers, onions, garlic, and ginger. Sauté, stirring frequently, only until peppers are half done, Chinese style. Remove from fire. Stir in soy sauce, nutmeg, and cloves, blending well. Add salt, pepper, and sugar to taste. Chill.

❡ Preheat electric skillet or griddle at 300 degrees. Brush lightly with oil. Sauté hamburgers until medium brown on both sides. Place peppers in a lightly greased skillet and sauté only until heated through. Spoon peppers over hamburgers on serving platter or pass separately at table.

Lamb Kebabs with Mustard Sauce

4 pound half leg of lamb
6 tablespoons prepared mild mustard
2 tablespoons heavy cream
Salt
Pepper
1½ cups milk
4 tablespcons instant dissolving flour
4 tablespoons butter
2 hard-boiled egg yolks
½ cup sour cream
2 teaspoons lemon juice
2 teaspoons dry mustard
2 tablespoons milk

Have butcher bone leg of lamb and cut it into 1 inch squares ½ inch thick. Mix 6 tablespoons prepared mustard and heavy cream. Fasten lamb on skewers. Sprinkle with salt and pepper. Brush with mustard mixture. Chill. Pour 1½ cups milk into saucepan. Add flour and stir until flour dissolves. Add butter. Bring to a boil over a moderate flame, stirring constantly, until sauce is thick. Reduce flame and simmer 5 minutes. Remove sauce from fire. Force egg yolks through a fine wire sieve. Add to sauce. Add sour cream and lemon juice. Stir well. Dissolve dry mustard in 2 tablespoons milk and stir into sauce. Add salt and pepper to taste. Cover sauce with tight-fitting lid. Chill.

¶ Preheat broiler flame or prepare charcoal fire for broiling. Broil lamb until brown on two sides. It is best if cooked somewhat rare, with a little pink showing in the center of the meat. Heat sauce in top section of double boiler over simmering water. Stir frequently. Pass sauce to pour over meat, and over rice if served as an accompaniment.

Baked Peppers Stuffed with Ham and Chicken

4 large sweet green peppers
¾ pound Virginia style baked ham,
    thinly sliced
½ pound chicken or turkey roll,
    thinly sliced
4 ounce can mushroom pieces
    and stems
2½ cups chicken broth
¾ cup butter or margarine
½ cup very finely minced onions

¾ cup flour
1 tablespoon very finely minced
    parsley
1 teaspoon dried summer savory
1 tablespoon lemon juice
Salt
Pepper
Bread crumbs
Grated parmesan cheese
Salad oil

Place peppers, one or two at a time, directly over a gas flame, turning occasionally until peppers are blistery black. Rinse under cold running water. Rub with a coarse towel to remove as much as possible of the thin outer skin. Set aside. Chop ham and chicken very fine. Drain mushrooms, reserving juice. Chop mushrooms very fine. Combine mushroom juice and chicken broth. Heat up to boiling point but do not boil. Melt butter or margarine in another saucepan. Add onions. Sauté until onions are yellow but not brown. Stir in flour, blending well. Slowly stir in chicken broth mixture. Bring to a boil. Reduce flame and simmer 5 minutes. Add ham, chicken, mushrooms, parsley, and savory. Simmer 5 minutes. Add lemon juice and salt and pepper to taste. Chill slightly. Cut peppers through stem end. Remove seeds, stems, and inner membrane. Stuff peppers with ham mixture. Sprinkle top first with bread crumbs, then with cheese, coating top well. Place on a greased shallow baking pan. Chill.

❦ Preheat oven at 375 degrees. Sprinkle peppers with salad oil. Bake 30 minutes.

6 THE MIDNIGHT COOKBOOK

Veal Balls with Deviled Tomato Sauce

2 pounds boneless shoulder of veal
1 large onion
1 large carrot
1 bay leaf
Salt
Pepper
1 cup butter or margarine
½ cup very finely minced onions
½ teaspoon oregano
Flour
4 ounce can mushroom pieces and
stems

1 tablespoon very finely minced
parsley
2 tablespoons lemon juice
2 eggs, beaten
¼ cup milk
Bread crumbs
2 cans (8 ounces each) tomato sauce
2 tablespoons vinegar
¼ cup bottled sauce diable
Deep fat for frying

Cover veal with cold water in a soup pot. Add whole onion, carrot, bay leaf, and 2 teaspoons salt. Simmer 1½ hours or until very tender. Strain stock and reserve. When veal is cool enough to handle, cut it first into very thin slices, removing all fat and gristle. Then cut veal into tiny dice no larger than $\frac{1}{16}$ inch. Melt butter or margarine in a saucepan. Add ½ cup minced onions and oregano. Sauté until onions are yellow but not brown. Stir in 1 cup flour with wire whip, blending well. Drain liquid from mushrooms. Add enough veal stock to mushroom liquid to make 1 quart. Slowly stir stock into flour mixture. Bring to a boil. Reduce flame and simmer 5 minutes. Cut mushrooms into pieces no larger than the veal. Add veal and mushrooms to sauce. Simmer 5 minutes. Add parsley, lemon juice, and salt and pepper to taste. Chill well. Shape into balls no larger than 1 inch in diameter. Mix eggs and milk. Dip veal balls in flour, then in eggs, and then in bread crumbs, coating thoroughly. Chill. In a saucepan mix tomato sauce, vinegar, and sauce diable. Chill.

❡ Preheat deep fat at 370 degrees. Fry veal balls until medium brown, doing job in several batches. Sprinkle veal balls with salt. Heat sauce over moderate flame until bubbling hot. Pass sauce separately at table.

Sesame Meatballs with Sweet-and-Sour Sauce

1 pound ground beef
½ pound ground pork
½ pound ground veal
½ cup sesame seeds
½ cup salad oil
Soy sauce
2 tablespoons honey
¼ cup dry sherry
1 teaspoon onion powder
2 slices stale white bread

1 medium-size onion
2 eggs, slightly beaten
Salt
Pepper
4 cups chicken broth, fresh or
    canned
1½ cups brown sugar firmly packed
1 cup cider vinegar
½ cup catsup
6 tablespoons cornstarch

Place sesame seeds in heavy pan over moderate flame. Heat, stirring frequently, until seeds are brown but not scorched. Place in blender and blend until pulverized. Mix seeds with oil, ½ cup soy sauce, honey, sherry, and onion powder. Set aside. Dip bread in water and squeeze gently to remove excess water. Break into small pieces. Place meat in mixing bowl with bread. Grate onion into bowl. Add eggs, 1 teaspoon salt, and ¼ teaspoon pepper. Mix extremely well, breaking up bread as much as possible. Shape meat into balls 1 inch in diameter. Marinate balls in sesame mixture ½ hour. Remove from marinade and place balls in single layer in a shallow baking pan. Preheat oven at 400 degrees. Bake balls, turning once to brown evenly, 30 to 40 minutes. Mix chicken broth, brown sugar, vinegar, 1 tablespoon soy sauce, and catsup in saucepan. Dissolve cornstarch in ¼ cup cold water. Bring chicken broth mixture to a boil. Slowly stir in cornstarch. Simmer 2 to 3 minutes. Combine meatballs and sauce in large shallow saucepan. Chill.

❦ Reheat over low flame or in top of double boiler, stirring but keeping meatballs intact. Serve with boiled noodles or rice Chinese style. Pass hot Chinese mustard at table.

Chicken Curry with Mint

4 whole breasts of chicken (8 halves), skinless and boneless
¼ cup butter
½ cup very finely minced onions
¼ cup very finely minced green pepper
1 teaspoon very finely minced fresh ginger
1 teaspoon very finely minced hot chili pepper
2 teaspoons ground cumin
½ teaspoon ground coriander
½ teaspoon ground fennel
1 teaspoon turmeric
3 cups medium cream sauce (see page 50)
2 envelopes instant chicken broth
4 tablespoons medium dry sherry
4 teaspoons very finely chopped fresh mint
Salt
Pepper
1 cup yogurt

NOTE: If fresh ginger isn't available, preserved ginger in syrup may be substituted.

Cut away gristle in center of chicken breasts. Separate breasts into halves. Cut breasts crosswise into ¼ inch slices. Set aside. Melt butter in a heavy saucepan. Add onions, green pepper, ginger, chili pepper, cumin, coriander, fennel, and turmeric. Stir well. Sauté only until onions are tender. Add chicken. Saute covered only until chicken loses raw color. Add cream sauce, instant broth, sherry, and mint. Simmer 5 minutes, stirring frequently. Add salt and pepper to taste. Chill.

❡ Reheat in top part of double boiler over simmering water. When curry is hot, stir in yogurt. Correct seasoning if necessary. Heat a few minutes longer before serving.

Skewered Chicken with Red Radish Dip

4 whole chicken breasts (8 halves), boneless and skinless
2 medium-size cloves garlic
2 medium-size onions, thinly sliced
3 tablespoons lemon juice
Salad oil
Salt
Pepper
Bread crumbs
½ cup shredded red radishes
¾ cup mayonnaise
¾ cup sour cream
2 teaspoons finely chopped fresh chives

Cut chicken into pieces ¾ inch square or as close to that size as possible. Peel garlic and mash lightly but do not chop. In a mixing bowl combine chicken, onions, garlic, 2 tablespoons lemon juice, and ¼ cup salad oil. Toss ingredients well. Cover bowl and chill 3 to 4 hours. Remove chicken from onion mixture. Fasten chicken on 8 skewers, folding chicken before fastening if necessary to keep pieces compact on skewer. Sprinkle with salt and pepper. Dip in bread crumbs. Chill. Shred red radishes by forcing them through large holes of square metal grater. Mix mayonnaise, sour cream, radishes, chives, and remaining 1 tablespoon lemon juice. Add salt and pepper if desired. Chill.

❦ Preheat broiler. Dab chicken lightly with oil, using a pastry brush. Broil until medium brown on both sides. Serve with radish dip.

Baked Tomatoes with Chicken Hash and Melted Cheddar Cheese

2½-pound chicken, boiled
4 large firm ripe beefsteak tomatoes
2½ cups potatoes cut in medium dice
2 tablespoons butter or margarine
⅓ cup very finely minced onion
1 teaspoon very finely minced garlic
1 teaspoon very finely minced hot chili pepper
2 tablespoons heavy cream
2 teaspoons worcestershire sauce
Salt
Pepper
6 ounces sharp cheddar cheese, thinly sliced

Remove skin and bones from boiled chicken. Cut into extremely small dice or chop as for hash. Boil potatoes in salted water until tender. Mash half the potatoes. Chop balance of potatoes so that pieces are approximately the same size as the chicken. Melt butter in a saucepan. Add onion, garlic, and chili pepper. Sauté until onion is yellow but not brown. Turn chicken, potatoes, and onion mixture into a mixing bowl. Add heavy cream, worcestershire sauce, and salt and pepper to taste. Mix well. Mixture should be firm enough so that it can be shaped by hand. If it is too loose, add a few tablespoons bread crumbs. Cut tomatoes in half horizontally. Sprinkle cut side of tomatoes with salt and pepper. Place a mound of chicken hash on top of each half tomato. Place tomatoes in a greased shallow baking pan. Chill.

❡ Preheat oven at 375 degrees. Bake 25 minutes. Place a slice of cheese, large enough to cover each portion, on top of chicken hash. Bake 5 minutes longer or until cheese is melted.

Chicken Timbales with Pimiento Sauce

3-pound chicken, boiled, or 1½ pounds chicken or turkey roll,
   very thinly sliced
6 cups stale bread cubes without crust
2 cups chicken broth
¾ cup milk
6 egg yolks, well beaten
⅓ cup melted butter or margarine
1 medium-size onion
Salt
Pepper
2 cups rich cream sauce (see page 50)
½ cup light cream
2 jars (2 ounces each) sliced pimientos
1 tablespoon very finely minced parsley

Remove skin and bones from chicken. Chop chicken very fine. Put bread cubes in several batches into blender and blend at high speed until crumbs are formed. There should be approximately 2¼ cups crumbs. Add or subtract crumbs if necessary to make this amount. In a mixing bowl combine bread crumbs, chicken broth, milk, egg yolks, and melted butter or margarine. Mix well. Add chicken. Grate onion into bowl. Add 1 teaspoon salt and ¼ teaspoon pepper. Mix well. Preheat oven at 375 degrees. Grease well 8 custard cups or timbale molds of equivalent size. Spoon chicken mixture into cups. Place in a deep baking pan. Add 1 inch very hot water. Bake 25 to 30 minutes or until timbales are firm when lightly touched. Remove from pan. Chill. Mix cream sauce, light cream, pimientos, and parsley. Add salt and pepper to taste. Chill.

❡ Preheat over at 375 degrees. Again place timbales in deep baking pan. Add 1 inch very hot water. Bake 20 minutes. Reheat sauce over moderate flame or in top part of double boiler over simmering water. Run a knife along inside of each custard cup. Unmold onto platter or serving plates. Pour sauce on top.

Coconut Chicken with Spiced Bananas

3½-pound chicken, boiled
1 pound fresh mushrooms
Butter
2 cans (4 ounces each) shredded
   coconut
3 cups milk
½ cup light cream
6 tablespoons flour

Salt
Pepper
8 medium-size ripe bananas
Orange juice
¼ cup sugar
1 teaspoon cinnamon
½ teaspoon ground mace
½ teaspoon ground coriander

Remove skin and bones from chicken. Cut into ¾ inch dice. If mushrooms are large cut into halves or quarters. Cut again into thin slices. Melt 2 tablespoons butter in skillet. Sauté mushrooms until tender and until all mushroom liquid has evaporated from pan. Set aside. Put coconut, milk, and cream in a saucepan. Over a very low flame, bring up to the boiling point but do not boil. Let coconut milk remain in saucepan ½ hour. When coconut milk is cool enough to handle, force it through a double thickness of cheesecloth. Discard coconut. Return coconut milk to a saucepan. Again bring up to a boil, but do not boil. In another saucepan melt 6 tablespoons butter over a low flame. Slowly stir in flour, blending well with a wire whip. Slowly stir in coconut milk, blending well. Bring up to a boil. Reduce flame and simmer 5 minutes, stirring frequently. Add mushrooms and chicken. Simmer 5 minutes. Season lightly with salt and pepper. Chill. Peel bananas and cut crosswise in half. Dip in orange juice to prevent discoloration. Melt 4 tablespoons butter and brush on bananas. In a small bowl mix sugar, cinnamon, mace, and coriander. Dip bananas in sugar mixture, coating evenly. Place bananas on a greased shallow baking sheet. Chill. A few hours in the refrigerator will not harm the bananas.

❧ Preheat oven at 375 degrees. Bake bananas 15 to 20 minutes or until tender. Reheat chicken in top part of double boiler over simmering water. Place bananas on chicken in serving dish or casserole.

Chicken and Mushrooms with Lemon Cream Sauce

4-pound chicken, boiled
1 pound fresh mushrooms
Butter
1 cup cold light cream
1 cup cold milk
1/3 cup instant dissolving flour
2 cups chicken broth
1 tablespoon very finely minced dill
1/4 cup very finely minced scallions, white part only
2 tablespoons very finely minced parsley
Salt
Pepper
4 egg yolks
3 tablespoons lemon juice

Cut mushrooms into 1/2 inch dice. Sauté in 3 tablespoons butter until tender. Set aside. Remove skin and bones from chicken. Cut chicken into 1/2 inch dice. Pour cream and milk into a large saucepan. Stir in 1/3 cup flour until flour dissolves. Add chicken broth and 1/3 cup butter. Cook over a moderate flame, stirring constantly, until sauce is thick. Reduce flame and simmer 5 minutes. Add chicken and mushrooms. Simmer 5 minutes. Add dill, scallions, and parsley, and salt and pepper to taste. Chill.

❡ Reheat chicken in top part of double boiler over simmering water. Stir occasionally. When sauce is hot, beat egg yolks and lemon juice together. Add a few tablespoons sauce to lemon mixture. Slowly stir lemon mixture into chicken. Heat about 5 minutes, stirring frequently. Correct seasoning if necessary.

Creamed Chicken, Mushrooms, and Onions with Curry Biscuits

3½-pound chicken, boiled
3 cans (4 ounces each) mushroom stems and pieces
2 cups cold chicken broth
Light cream
½ cup instant dissolving flour
½ cup butter or margarine
Salt
Pepper
2 cans (8 ounces each) small white onions
4 tablespoons medium dry sherry

Remove skin and bones from chicken. Cut into ½ inch dice. Drain mushrooms, reserving juice. Combine mushroom juice and chicken broth. Add enough light cream to the chicken broth mixture to make 1 quart liquid. Pour into heavy saucepan. Stir in flour until flour dissolves completely. Add butter or margarine. Heat over a moderate flame, stirring constantly, until sauce is thick. Reduce flame and simmer 5 minutes, stirring frequently. Add salt and pepper to taste. If sauce seems weak, add 2 or 3 packets instant chicken broth. Drain onions, discarding liquid. Add chicken, mushrooms, and onions to sauce. Simmer 10 minutes. Stir in sherry. Chill. Prepare biscuits following recipe on page 89, eliminating peppers and instead sifting 2 teaspoons curry powder and ½ teaspoon onion powder with dry ingredients.

❡ Reheat chicken in top part of double boiler over simmering water. Correct seasoning if necessary. Split curry biscuits in half. Spoon chicken between and over biscuit halves on serving plates.

Chicken and Oyster Pie

3-pound chicken, boiled
2 dozen medium to large size shucked oysters
2 eight-inch piecrusts, baked
½ pound mushrooms
Butter
1½ cups cold chicken broth
½ cup milk
½ cup instant dissolving flour
2 cups potatoes cut in ½ inch dice
Salt
Pepper
½ cup bread crumbs

Piecrusts should be baked a light rather than deep brown. Remove skin and bones from chicken. Cut into ½ inch dice. Cut mushrooms into ½ inch dice. Sauté mushrooms in 2 tablespoons butter until mushrooms are tender and no mushroom liquid remains in pan. Set aside. Pour chicken broth and milk into saucepan. Stir in flour until flour dissolves. Add ½ cup butter. Cook over a moderate flame, stirring constantly, until sauce is thick. Reduce flame and simmer 5 minutes, stirring occasionally. If sauce seems weak, 1 or 2 envelopes instant chicken broth may be added. Boil potatoes in salted water until tender. Drain. In another saucepan heat oysters in their own liquor only until edges of oysters curl. Drain oysters, discarding liquor. In a mixing bowl combine chicken, mushrooms, sauce, potatoes, and oysters. Add ¼ cup bread crumbs. Add salt and pepper to taste. Fill pie shells with chicken mixture. Sprinkle balance of bread crumbs evenly over pie fillings. Melt 2 tablespoons butter and sprinkle over bread crumbs. Chill.

❡ Preheat oven at 350 degrees. Bake pies 40 to 50 minutes.

Breaded Chicken Collops with Onion Sauce Au Gratin

4 whole chicken breasts (8 halves),
   skinless and boneless
Salt
Pepper
3 eggs
¼ cup milk
Flour
Bread crumbs
Salad oil

½ cup butter
4 cups sliced onions
½ cup flour
2 cups hot milk
2 cups hot chicken broth
1 cup light cream
1 cup sharp cheddar cheese,
   shredded
Grated parmesan cheese

Cut chicken breasts in half. Cut away gristle from center of each breast. Remove filet from underside of each breast. Cut balance of each breast in half lengthwise, making 3 pieces out of each breast. Sprinkle all chicken with salt and pepper. Beat eggs and ¼ cup milk. Dip chicken in flour, then in eggs, and then in bread crumbs, coating thoroughly. Heat ¼ inch oil in large skillet. Sauté chicken until light brown, replacing oil when necessary. Place chicken in clusters of 3 overlapping pieces to each portion on a greased shallow casserole or pan. Heat butter in a saucepan. Sauté onions, stirring frequently, only until onions are soft but not yellow. Remove from fire. Stir in flour, blending well. Slowly stir in 2 cups milk and chicken broth. Return to a moderate flame and bring to a boil. Add cream. Reduce flame and simmer 10 minutes, stirring frequently. Let sauce cool slightly. Place in blender in batches and blend smooth. Add salt and pepper to taste. Sprinkle cheddar cheese over chicken. Pour sauce over chicken. Sprinkle parmesan cheese on top. Chill.

❡ Preheat oven at 350 degrees. Bake 25 to 30 minutes.

Fried Chicken Quenelles with Watercress Dip

1½ pounds (trimmed weight)
   chicken breasts, boneless and
   skinless
⅓ cup sliced onions
1½ teaspoons salt
¼ teaspoon white pepper
2 eggs, whites and yolks separated
1 cup heavy cream

1 whole egg
3 tablespoons milk
Flour
Bread crumbs
½ cup heavy cream
1½ cups mayonnaise
¼ bunch watercress
Deep fat for frying

Cut away gristle in center of chicken breasts. Put chicken and onions through meat grinder twice, using fine blade. Place chicken, salt, and pepper in bowl of electric mixer. Beat egg whites slightly in a deep dish. Set mixer at low speed. Add egg whites, about 2 tablespoons at a time, beating well after each addition. Add 1 cup cream in the same manner. Chill mixture in refrigerator for about ½ hour. Fill a tablespoon with a rounded quantity (actually about 2 tablespoons) chicken mixture. Use a second tablespoon dipped in very hot water to make an oval-shaped quenelle and empty it into a greased shallow saucepan. Do not crowd pan. Continue in this manner until all chicken is used. Use several pans if necessary. Cover quenelles with boiling water. Sprinkle with salt. Cook, covered, about 12 minutes. Drain quenelles and dry on paper toweling. Chill slightly. Beat egg yolks with whole egg and milk. Dip quenelles in flour, then in beaten egg, and then in bread crumbs, coating thoroughly. Chill. Beat ½ cup cream until whipped. Fold into mayonnaise. Chop watercress very fine. Place in a clean towel and squeeze to eliminate as much liquid as possible. Fold watercress into mayonnaise mixture. Chill.

❡ Fry quenelles (do not overload frying basket) in deep fat preheated at 370 degrees. Pass watercress dip separately at table.

Skewered Chicken and Pineapple with Chili Dip

4 whole breasts of chicken (8 halves), boneless and skinless
1 can (20 ounces) pineapple chunks, drained
Salt
Pepper
½ cup melted butter or margarine
Prepared mild mustard
Bread crumbs
1 cup mayonnaise
⅓ cup sweet pickle relish
2 teaspoons chili powder
2 tablespoons heavy cream

Remove long strip or filet from underside of each chicken breast. Cut filets in half crosswise. Cut balance of chicken in pieces approximately the same size. Sprinkle chicken with salt and pepper. Fold each piece of chicken, and fasten chicken and pineapple alternately on skewers. Brush chicken and pineapple with melted butter or margarine. Brush chicken pieces lightly with mustard. Dip skewers in bread crumbs, coating thoroughly. Place skewers on greased shallow pans. Chill. Mix mayonnaise, pickle relish, chili powder, and cream, adding more chili powder if desired. Chill.

❏ Preheat broiler. Drizzle melted butter or salad oil on chicken. Broil, turning once, until chicken is medium brown. Pass chili dip separately at table.

Chicken Balls with Horseradish and Caper Sauce

2 pounds (trimmed weight) boneless and skinless chicken breasts
3 cups stale bread cut in ½ inch cubes
1 medium-size onion, sliced
2 eggs, beaten
2 teaspoons salt
¼ teaspoon white pepper
⅛ teaspoon freshly grated nutmeg
½ cup butter
½ cup flour
Salt
Pepper
4 teaspoons prepared horseradish
4 teaspoons small capers in vinegar, drained

Separate whole chicken breasts in halves. Cut away gristle in center of breasts. Cut chicken into large cubes. Soak bread in cold water, pressing gently to remove excess water. Put chicken, onion, and bread cubes through meat grinder twice, using fine blade. In a mixing bowl combine ground chicken mixture, eggs, 2 teaspoons salt, ¼ teaspoon white pepper, and nutmeg, mixing well. Chill mixture slightly. Shape into balls no larger than 1 inch in diameter. Dip hands in cold water to shape balls. Bring 2 quarts water and 1 teaspoon salt to a boil in a large saucepan or dutch oven. Add chicken balls in several batches and simmer 5 minutes after chicken balls rise to top. Remove balls from pan. Measure 1 quart liquid in which chicken balls were cooked and set aside. In a saucepan melt butter. Stir in flour, blending well. Slowly stir in reserved cooking liquid. Bring to a boil. Reduce flame and simmer 5 minutes, stirring frequently. If sauce seems weak in flavor, add powdered instant chicken bouillon to taste. Add horseradish, capers, and salt and pepper to taste. Add chicken balls. Chill.

❡ Reheat in double boiler over simmering water.

Chinese Chicken with Grapes and Almonds

4 whole chicken breast (8 halves),
  boneless and skinless
2 eggs
M.S.G. seasoning
Salt
Pepper
Cornstarch
Soy sauce
Peanut oil
½ teaspoon very finely minced garlic

½ teaspoon very finely minced fresh
  ginger
2 tablespoons very finely minced
  onion
2¼ cups chicken broth
6 tablespoons vinegar
6 tablespoons sugar
¼ cup catsup
½ cup thinly sliced almonds
2 cups seedless grapes

Cut each chicken breast in half. Cut away gristle in center of breast. Separate filets from underside of each breast. Cut each filet crosswise into thirds. Cut balance of chicken about the same size. Flatten all chicken with a meat mallet; avoid tearing pieces of chicken. Prepare a batter by beating until smooth the eggs, 1 teaspoon M.S.G. seasoning, 1 teaspoon salt, 6 tablespoons cornstarch, and ½ teaspoon soy sauce. Heat peanut oil to a depth of ¼ inch in a large skillet or wok. Dip chicken in batter. Sauté the chicken, stirring well to keep pieces of chicken from sticking together, until chicken is medium brown. Lift chicken from pan and drain well. Chill. Heat 2 tablespoons oil in saucepan. Sauté garlic, ginger, and onion a few seconds; do not brown. Add chicken broth, vinegar, sugar, catsup, 1 teaspoon M.S.G. seasoning, and 1 teaspoon soy sauce. Bring to a boil. Dissolve 2 tablespoons cornstarch in 2 tablespoons cold water. Stir into sauce. Simmer 2 minutes. Add salt and pepper to taste. Chill. Preheat oven at 375 degrees. Place almonds in a shallow pan. Bake about 10 minutes or until lightly browned.

❆ Preheat oven at 350 degrees. Bake chicken in a shallow pan 5 to 8 minutes. Combine sauce and grapes in saucepan. Heat over a moderate flame. Pour bubbling hot sauce over chicken on serving plates or casserole. Sprinkle with almonds.

Chinese Chicken Velvet with Virginia Ham

4 whole chicken breasts (8 halves), skinless and boneless
12 ounces country style Virginia ham, thinly sliced
4 egg whites
M.S.G. seasoning
Salt
Pepper
Soy sauce
½ cup cornstarch
½ cup peanut oil
2 teaspoons sesame oil

NOTE: This is a moist dish without sauce and may be served with another Chinese dish that has a sauce, if desired.

Cut each chicken breast in half. Cut away gristle in center of each breast. Separate filets from underside of each breast. Cut each filet crosswise into thirds. Cut balance of chicken about the same size. Flatten with a meat mallet or side of a cleaver; avoid tearing chicken. Cut chicken with a cleaver or heavy French knife into thinnest possible strips. Beat egg whites, 2 teaspoons M.S.G. seasoning, 2 teaspoons salt, 1 teaspoon soy sauce, and cornstarch until mixture is smooth. Dip chicken into mixture. Bring a large pot of water to a rapid boil. Add coated chicken. Stir well. Cook only until water comes to a second boil, stirring frequently to separate pieces of chicken. Drain chicken. Heat peanut oil and sesame oil in a large skillet or wok. Add chicken. Sauté a few minutes, stirring constantly, only until chicken is heated through. Remove chicken from pan. Do not wash pan. Chicken should be glossy with oil but not brown. Add salt and pepper to taste, and more soy sauce and M.S.G. seasoning if desired. Cut ham into very thin strips about 1 inch long. Place ham in pan in which chicken was cooked and sauté only until light brown. Add ham to chicken. Chill.

❆ Reheat in top part of double boiler over simmering water. Serve very hot.

Breast of Chicken with Provolone and Bacon

4 whole breasts of chicken (8 halves), boneless and skinless
8 slices bacon
4 ounces provolone cheese, sliced
Salt
Pepper
Flour
3 eggs, beaten
Bread crumbs
Salad oil
3 cups medium cream sauce (see page 50)
3 tablespoons very finely minced fresh or 1 teaspoon dried oregano
3 tablespoons very finely chopped shallots or scallions, white part only
2 tablespoons medium dry sherry

Panfry the bacon until it is medium brown, but not so crisp that it is brittle. Remove long strip or filet from underside of each chicken breast. Flatten the filet gently with a meat mallet; do not hit it so hard that it tears. Place a narrow strip of provolone cheese where the filet was removed. Place a strip of bacon on the cheese. Place filet on top to cover bacon and cheese. Pat filet down firmly. Prepare all breasts in the same manner. Sprinkle with salt and pepper. Holding each portion of chicken with two hands to keep pieces intact, dip in flour, eggs, and bread crumbs. Pat bread crumbs into chicken to make a firm coating. Heat ¼ inch salad oil in large skillet. Sauté chicken, turning each portion carefully, only until bread crumbs are lightly colored. They should not be deeply browned. Place chicken on a greased shallow pan. Chill. Mix cream sauce, oregano, shallots or scallions, and sherry in a saucepan. Simmer 5 minutes. Cover and chill.

❦ Preheat oven at 375 degrees. Bake chicken 20 minutes. Reheat sauce over low flame. Sauce may be thinned with a little light cream or milk if desired. Pour sauce on serving plates and place chicken on top, or pass separately at table.

Breast of Chicken with Smothered Onions

4 whole breasts of chicken (8 halves), boneless and skinless
2 eggs, beaten
2 tablespoons heavy cream
2 Spanish onions, about 12 ounces each
Salt
Pepper
Flour
Salad oil
2 tablespoons butter
1 teaspoon meat extract
Sugar
1 cup dry white wine
1¼ cups canned sauce bordelaise or canned brown sauce

Cut chicken breasts into halves. Cut away gristle in center of breasts. Flatten breasts slightly with meat mallet or side of a cleaver. Mix eggs and cream. Peel onions and cut in half through stem end. Cut crosswise into thinnest possible slices. Break slices apart to make strips. Sprinkle chicken with salt and pepper. Dip in flour, coating thoroughly. Dip in eggs. Heat ¼ inch oil in a large skillet. Sauté chicken until medium brown on both sides. Place chicken on a well-greased shallow pan. Heat butter and 1 tablespoon oil in a large saucepan. Sauté onions, stirring frequently, until onions are deep yellow. Add meat extract. Stir well. Add salt and pepper and a dash of sugar. Add wine. Cook until wine is reduced to about half its original quantity. Add sauce. Simmer slowly 10 minutes. Correct seasoning if necessary. Spoon onions on chicken. Chill.

❡ Preheat oven at 375 degrees. Bake chicken 15 minutes. Serve on toast or fried bread.

Paprika Chicken with Yogurt

3½-pound chicken, boiled
2 cups diced fresh tomatoes
½ cup butter or margarine
½ cup green peppers cut in small dice
¼ cup finely minced onions
4 teaspoons paprika
1 teaspoon creole seasoning
⅔ cup flour
1 quart hot chicken broth
1½ cups yogurt
Salt
Pepper

Remove skin and bones from chicken and cut chicken into ½ inch dice. Lower tomatoes into boiling water for about 20 seconds; peel and remove stem end. Cut tomatoes into sixths, press to remove all seeds, and cut into ½ inch dice. Melt butter or margarine in a heavy saucepan. Add green peppers and onions. Sauté over low flame until onions are tender but not brown. Stir in paprika and creole seasoning. Add tomatoes. Cook until tomatoes are tender. Remove from fire. Stir in flour, blending well until no dry flour is visible. Slowly stir in chicken broth. Return to a moderate flame and simmer 10 minutes, stirring frequently. Taste sauce; if it seems weak add 2 or 3 packets instant chicken broth. Add chicken. Simmer over very low flame 10 minutes. Add salt and pepper to taste. Remove from fire. Stir in yogurt, blending well. Chill.

❦ Reheat in top part of double boiler over simmering water. Correct seasoning if necessary.

8

Cold Dishes and Salads

COLD DISHES AND SALADS no longer need wait for the summer. For late supper parties, a cold board is as appetizing in January as in July. From the hostess' standpoint, the most obvious advantage is that she can serve her platter or salad from the refrigerator while still wearing an evening gown. At posttheater parties, when guests may have had only a snack for dinner earlier in the evening, the cold platter or cold salad supper is the fastest possible way of satisfying midnight hunger.

The appearance of a cold dish or salad, its look of freshness and natural color, is almost as important as the taste of the food itself in the mouth. This doesn't mean that every cold dish must be elaborately decorated, beneath aspics, or otherwise affectedly made to look like a dish competing for the *décorateur*'s prize at a chefs' convention. But the food, neat but not gaudy, should be brought to the table on the handsomest platter or serving dish available. You can improvise tasteful garnishes to add to the platter's eye appeal.

Not only the appearance but the seasonings of cold foods must be vivid, since foods that have been chilled do not offer the enticing aromas of hot foods. Cold dishes should be really cold and not taken from the refrigerator until just before they're served. They will be most appreciated if they are served on cold dinner plates, which may be prechilled for a few minutes in the freezer. At this kind of gathering, an assortment of breads and fresh sweet butter should be within easy reach of all.

Cold Chicken and Ham with Tarragon Sauce

4 whole breasts of chicken
  (8 halves), skinless and boneless
4 slices (1¼ ounces each) boneless
  ham roll
2½ cup chicken broth, fresh or
  canned
2 tablespoons fresh tarragon leaves
  coarsely chopped

4 tablespoons flour
2 teaspoons tarragon vinegar
1 envelope plain gelatin
Salt
Pepper
24 fresh large tarragon leaves
¼ cup canned jellied madrilene

NOTE: Dried tarragon cannot be used successfully in this dish.

Melt 2 tablespoons butter in large skillet. Sauté ham slices until lightly browned around edges. Avoid overcooking. Cut ham slices in half and place in a single layer in a shallow casserole or on a large platter. If chicken breasts are whole, cut into halves and cut away gristle in center of breast. Place chicken in a single layer in a saucepan or dutch oven. Add chicken broth and chopped tarragon. Bring to a boil. Reduce flame, cover pan with tight-fitting lid, and simmer, don't boil, 10 minutes. Remove chicken from pan. Place on top of ham. Strain broth and set aside. Melt remaining 4 tablespoons butter in saucepan. Stir in flour until well blended. Slowly stir in strained chicken broth and simmer 5 minutes. Add tarragon vinegar. Soften gelatin in ¼ cup cold water. Remove sauce from fire and stir in softened gelatin. Add salt and pepper to taste. Pour over chicken. Chill. When sauce is almost jelled, arrange 3 whole tarragon leaves diagonally on each chicken breast. Chill. Cool madrilene in refrigerator until it is syrupy looking but not jelled. If madrilene is completely jelled, let it stand at room temperature until it is syrupy looking. Brush madrilene on chicken and on sauce between pieces of chicken. Chill until serving time.

Cold Filet of Beef with Watercress and Potato Salad

6 to 7 pound filet of beef
Salad oil
Salt
Pepper
½ teaspoon beef extract
1 cup beef stock
1 tablespoon Madeira or medium dry
   sherry
3 pounds potatoes

¼ cup red wine vinegar
2 tablespoons very finely minced
   chives
1 egg yolk
1 teaspoon Dijon mustard
½ teaspoon dry mustard
1 bunch watercress, washed and
   well drained
2 hard-boiled eggs, chopped fine

For best results, roast filet of beef about 6 to 8 hours before it is to be served. Filet will then still have its fresh beef flavor rather than the tired flavor of meat refrigerated overnight. Have filet trimmed of all fat, ready for roasting. Remove from the refrigerator while still wearing an evening gown. At post-theater parties, with salad oil. Sprinkle with salt and pepper. Roast in a shallow pan 30 to 40 minutes. Remove meat from pan and place on platter. Chill. Add beef extract, stock, and Madeira or sherry to pan. Scrape pan to loosen drippings. Cook over top flame until gravy comes to a boil. Remove from fire. Add to the gravy any drippings from meat on platter. Boil potatoes until tender. Drain. As soon as potatoes are cool enough to handle, peel and cut into ½ inch cubes. Combine potatoes and gravy in a bowl and chill several hours. Toss potatoes several times to marinate in gravy as much as possible. Put 1 cup oil, vinegar, chives, egg yolk, both kinds of mustard, 1 teaspoon salt, and ¼ teaspoon pepper in blender. Blend smooth. Drain potatoes. Add oil mixture to potatoes. Again chill.

❦ Carve filet into slices ¼ inch thick. Sprinkle with salt. Place potatoes, watercress, and chopped egg in salad bowl. Toss well. Add salt and pepper to taste. Pass cold filet and salad separately at table.

Smoked Pork Butt with Celery Knob and Pepper Salad, Curry Dressing

2 pound smoked boneless pork butt
1½ pounds celery knobs
2 cups cabbage cut in ½ inch dice
1 medium-size sweet green pepper
1 medium-size sweet red pepper
8½ ounce can crushed pineapple
1½ cups mayonnaise
1 tablespoon curry powder

⅓ cup light cream
1 tablespoon cider vinegar
Salt
Pepper
Boston lettuce
1 bunch watercress, washed and well
   drained
2 tablespoons finely minced chives

Boil pork butt in unsalted water until tender, 1½ to 2 hours. Save cooking liquid. When pork butt is cool, cut into very thin slices. Cut slices into ½ inch squares. Remove root ends from celery knobs (also known as celeriac), peel, and boil whole 20 to 30 minutes, or until tender. Cut into thinnest possible slices. Cut slices into ½ inch squares. Place cabbage in a pot. Cover with part of the stock in which pork butt was cooked. Bring liquid up to a boil. Remove cabbage from liquid as soon as it boils. Drain well. Cut peppers lengthwise into quarters. Remove stem ends and inner membranes. Cut peppers crosswise into thinnest possible slices. Place pork butt, celery knobs, cabbage, and peppers in large mixing bowl. Drain pineapple well, pressing to remove excess liquid. Combine mayonnaise, curry powder, cream, vinegar, and pineapple. Mix well. Add mayonnaise mixture to pork butt mixture. Blend well, adding salt and pepper to taste. Line a serving platter with lettuce. Arrange salad in an oblong mound in center of platter. Place sprigs of watercress around salad. Sprinkle salad with chives. Chill until serving time.

Cold Salmon Trout in Cream

8 slices salmon trout, 6 to 8 ounces each
1 cup onions sliced very thin
½ cup shredded carrots
½ cup shredded celery
3 tablespoons butter
1 bay leaf
1 cup dry white wine
Salt
Pepper
1 cup heavy cream
½ cup milk
2 tablespoons Dijon mustard
4 tablespoons lemon juice
Cayenne pepper

Cut onions in half through stem end, then cut crosswise into thinnest possible slices. Break slices apart to make strips. Peel carrots and force through large holes of metal grater. Peel celery and force through large holes of metal grater. Do not use broken, odd pieces of celery. Melt butter in a saucepan or skillet large enough to accommodate the fish in a single layer. Add onions, carrots, celery, and bay leaf and sauté over low heat until onions just begin to turn yellow. Place fish in pan. Add wine and enough water barely to cover fish. Add 1 teaspoon salt and ¼ teaspoon pepper. Cook covered over low heat 10 to 12 minutes. Remove fish from pan and place in a shallow casserole for serving. To the liquid in the pan add the cream, milk, and mustard. Blend well with wire whip. Bring up to the boiling point but do not boil. Add lemon juice. Blend well. Add salt and pepper to taste and a dash of cayenne. Pour liquid and vegetables over fish. Chill until serving time.

Cold Lemon Sole and Roast Peppers with Mustard Dressing

2 pounds filet of lemon sole (small
   filets)
7½ ounce jar roasted sweet peppers,
   drained
Salt
Pepper
4 tablespoons lemon juice
1 tablespoon dry mustard
2 tablespoons prepared mild mustard

6 tablespoons sugar
6 tablespoons flour
¾ cup vinegar
3 eggs, beaten
1½ cups cold water
3 tablespoons butter
¾ cup milk
1½ teaspoons plain gelatin
1 cup Clamato

Cut each filet of sole in half lengthwise. Place a 1 inch square of roasted pepper on each piece of sole and roll up to enclose pepper. Fasten each roll with a toothpick. Place the fish in a single layer in a shallow pan. Sprinkle generously with salt and pepper. Cover with cold water. Add lemon juice. Bring to a boil, cover pan, and simmer slowly 10 minutes. In the top section of a double boiler mix both kinds of mustard, sugar, flour, and vinegar to a smooth paste. Slowly stir in eggs and 1½ cups cold water. If mixture is not smooth it may be put through a strainer. Add 1 teaspoon salt and ¼ teaspoon pepper. Place mixture over boiling water in a double boiler. Cook, stirring, until dressing is thick. Remove from heat. Stir in butter till butter melts. Slowly stir in milk. Remove sole from cooking liquid, drain each piece of excess liquid, and place on a large serving platter. Spoon the mustard dressing over the sole. Chill. When dressing is cold, dissolve gelatin in 3 tablespoons Clamato. Place over simmering water, stirring until gelatin dissolves. Stir in balance of Clamato. Set in refrigerator to chill. As soon as Clamato shows signs of jelling, brush or spoon it lightly over the sole without disturbing dressing. It should be applied as a clear, even coating over the fish, not in large blobs. Chill until serving time.

Cold Mackerel with Tomato and Fennel Sauce

4 mackerel, 1½ pounds each
Olive oil
Salt
Pepper
Bread crumbs
2 cups very thinly sliced onions
29 ounce can tomatoes with puree
1 teaspoon very finely minced garlic
¼ cup fennel chopped fine
1 teaspoon leaf thyme
1 teaspoon saffron crumbled
½ cup dry red wine
¼ cup red wine vinegar
2 tablespoons very finely minced parsley

This dish is best when made the day before it is served. Have mackerel split with backbone removed, each fish cut into two pieces, then cut crosswise to make 4 pieces of each fish. Preheat broiler. Brush each fish lightly with oil. Sprinkle with salt and pepper. Sprinkle with bread crumbs. Again sprinkle lightly with oil. Place fish on a greased shallow pan and broil, without turning, until light brown. Place fish in a single layer in a shallow casserole. Break onion slices into strips. Place tomatoes in a bowl and break or chop whole tomatoes into coarse pieces. Heat ¼ cup oil in a large saucepan. Add onions, garlic, fennel, thyme, and saffron. Sauté until onions are soft and yellow but not brown. Add wine and wine vinegar. Cook until liquid is reduced to about ¼ cup. Add tomatoes, ½ teaspoon salt, and ¼ teaspoon pepper. Stir well. Simmer 15 minutes. Correct seasoning if necessary. Spoon tomato mixture over mackerel. Chill until serving time.

❡ Sprinkle parsley over mackerel just before serving.

Cold Shrimp and Artichoke Hearts with Cream Dressing

2 pounds (cooked weight) shrimp, boiled, peeled, and deveined
  (4 pounds raw shrimp in shell)
2 cups thinly sliced cucumber
9 ounce package frozen artichoke hearts
2 egg yolks
3 tablespoons Dijon mustard
2 cups heavy sweet cream
3 tablespoons lemon juice
2 tablespoons very finely minced shallots or scallions,
  white part only
Salt
Pepper
1 tablespoon very finely minced parsley
1 tablespoon very finely minced chives

If possible, buy the small fresh Kirby "pickle" cucumbers. Peel. Cut in half lengthwise. If large cucumbers are used, cut in fourths lengthwise, and then cut crosswise
into thin slices. Cook artichoke hearts, following directions on package. Drain well.
Beat egg yolks slightly. Stir in mustard. Gradually stir in cream, lemon juice, and
shallots or scallions. Add shrimp, cucumber, and artichoke hearts. Add salt and
pepper to taste. Chill. Toss several times while shrimp are marinating.

❆ Serve in shallow casserole. Sprinkle with parsley and chives just before serving.

Cold Tomato Stuffed with Lobster, Egg, and Anchovy Dressing

4 live lobsters, 1¼ pounds each, boiled
8 large ripe summer beefsteak tomatoes
1 cup chili sauce
1 cup mayonnaise
1 tablespoon tarragon vinegar
1 teaspoon worcestershire sauce
¼ teaspoon Tabasco sauce

1 cup very finely minced celery
Salt
Pepper
8 hard-boiled eggs
3 tablespoons light cream
2 teaspoons anchovy paste
Boston lettuce
2 teaspoons very finely minced fresh chives

Lower tomatoes, 1 or 2 at a time, into rapidly boiling water for 20 seconds. Hold under cold running water briefly. Peel tomatoes. Remove stem ends. Cut each tomato vertically into 4 sections, starting at top and cutting about three-fourths of the way down. Do not cut all the way through; base of tomatoes should be intact so that "petals" do not come off. Separate sections slightly. Cut lobsters in half lengthwise. Remove stomach sac in back of head. Crack claws. Remove lobster meat and cut into ¼ inch dice. Do not discard tomalley and roe, if any. Mix chili sauce, ½ cup mayonnaise, vinegar, worcestershire sauce, and Tabasco sauce, blending well. Combine lobster, celery, and chili sauce mixture. Add salt and pepper to taste. Fill tomatoes with lobster mixture. Cut hard-boiled eggs into slices. Place one egg with slices overlapping on top each tomato. Chill. Mix remaining ½ cup mayonnaise with cream and anchovy paste, blending well. Chill.

❡ Place lettuce on serving platter. Carefully place tomatoes on lettuce. Spoon anchovy dressing over eggs. Sprinkle with chives.

Cold Stuffed Lobster Taiis with Apple

3 pounds small-size frozen lobster tails
2 cups apples cut in small dice
2 cups celery cut in small dice
1⅓ cups mayonnaise
2 tablespoons lemon juice
½ teaspoon sugar
4 teaspoons Dijon mustard
Salt
Pepper
1 cup mayonnaise
¼ cup catsup
1 tablespoon medium dry sherry
4 teaspoons prepared horseradish
1 tablespoon very finely minced fresh dill

Make sure there are at least 16 lobster tails. Boil lobster tails, following directions on package. When lobsters are cool enough to handle cut away soft undershell with scissors. Reserve shells. Remove lobster meat and cut into cubes no larger than ¼ inch. Peel and core apples. Peel celery with vegetable peeler. Cut celery and apples approximately same size as lobster. Mix lobster, apples, celery, 1⅓ cups mayonnaise, lemon juice, sugar, and mustard. Add salt and pepper, blending well. Bend lobster tails to flatten them for filling. Fill with lobster mixture. Chill. Mix 1 cup mayonnaise, catsup, sherry, and horseradish. Chill.

❡ Spoon mayonnaise and catsup mixture over lobster tails just before serving. Sprinkle with dill.

Avocado Stuffed with Ham Mousse

4 ripe medium-size avocados
1 lemon
1 pound baked or boiled ham, sliced
1 envelope plain gelatin
2 cups cold chicken broth, fresh or canned
¼ cup very finely chopped green pepper
¼ cup very finely chopped pimiento
2 tablespoons very finely chopped dill pickle
1 medium onion
½ cup mayonnaise
1 teaspoon Dijon mustard
2 teaspoons prepared horseradish
¼ teaspoon Tabasco sauce
1 tablespoon lemon juice
Salt
Pepper
¼ cup canned jellied madrilene

Put ham through meat grinder twice, using fine blade. Soften gelatin in ½ cup cold chicken broth. Place over hot water to dissolve. Add to remaining broth and stir well. Add ham, green pepper, pimiento, and pickle. Grate onion into mixture. Stir well. Place in refrigerator until mixture begins to jell and is no longer soupy; however, it must not be stiff. In a separate bowl mix mayonnaise, mustard, horseradish, Tabasco, and 1 tablespoon lemon juice. Fold mayonnaise mixture into ham mixture. Add salt and pepper to taste. Peel avocados and cut in half lengthwise. Sprinkle avocados inside and out with juice of lemon. Fill avocados with ham mousse, using a spatula to make a smooth mound over each avocado. Chill madrilene until it begins to jell. If it is completely jelled, let it stand at room temperature until it is syrupy looking. With a pastry brush dab each mound of mousse with madrilene. Chill until serving time.

Turkey, Tongue, and Bean Sprout Salad
with Mustard Cream Dressing

1 pound turkey roll or cooked breast of turkey, thinly sliced
1 pound cooked corned or smoked beef tongue, thinly sliced
1 pound can bean sprouts, well drained
2 cups Chinese cabbage julienne
½ cup green pepper julienne
1¼ cups mayonnaise
3 tablespoons prepared mild mustard
½ cup heavy cream
8 pickled walnuts, drained
2 jars (2 ounces each) pimiento strips
Boston lettuce
Salt
Pepper

Cut turkey and tongue into 1½ inch strips about ⅛ inch thick. Wash bean sprouts in cold water. Drain very well. Cut Chinese cabbage crosswise into thinnest possible slices. Cut green pepper in half through stem end. Remove seeds and inner white membrane. Cut crosswise into thinnest possible slices. In a large salad bowl toss bean sprouts, Chinese cabbage, and green pepper. Sprinkle turkey and tongue on top. Cover bowl with clear plastic wrap. Chill. Mix mayonnaise and mustard. Beat cream until whipped. Fold cream into mayonnaise mixture. Chill. Drain black walnuts and cut in half lengthwise. Chill. Drain pimiento strips. Chill.

❆ Line serving platter with lettuce leaves. Add dressing to salad and toss thoroughly. Add salt and pepper to taste. Place salad mixture on lettuce to form oblong mound. Arrange sliced walnuts and pimiento strips on top.

Corned Beef, Beet, Carrot, and Cabbage Salad

1½ pounds (cooked weight) cooked corned beef brisket, thinly sliced
16 ounce can beets julienne
2 cups boiled potatoes julienne
2 medium-size carrots, boiled
1 cup shredded cabbage
1 cup olive oil
⅓ cup red wine vinegar
½ teaspoon dry mustard
2 tablespoons finely chopped stuffed olives
¼ cup scallions, white part only, sliced very thin
2 tablespoons small capers in vinegar, drained
Salt
Pepper
2 large firm ripe tomatoes
Boston lettuce
10 ounce jar chowchow or piccalilli in mustard

Trim beef of as much fat as possible. Cut beef into strips about 1 inch long and ⅛ inch thick. Drain beets well. Cut potatoes and carrots into strips same size as beef. Shred cabbage on a coleslaw cutter or metal grater. In a small mixing bowl combine oil, vinegar, mustard, and 1 teaspoon salt. Beat with rotary beater. Stir in olives, scallions, and capers. In a large mixing bowl combine beef, beets, potatoes, cabbage, carrots, and olive oil mixture. Add salt and pepper to taste. Chill.

❦ Place salad in a mound on serving platter. Remove stem ends of tomatoes and cut each tomato into 4 slices. Place 8 inner leaves of lettuce around salad as "cups" for garnish. In each lettuce cup place a slice of tomato and alongside the tomato several small spoonfuls of chowchow.

Beef, Onion, Leek, and Potato Salad

3 pounds (raw weight) fresh brisket of
   beef, boiled and chilled
1½ cups leeks julienne
2 cups medium-size onions sliced thin
¼ cup olive oil
2 tablespoons white or red wine
   vinegar
½ cup sour gherkins julienne
2 cups boiled potatoes julienne
¾ cup mayonnaise

1 teaspoon Dijon mustard
1 tablespoon finely minced shallots or
   scallions, white part only
2 tablespoons very finely minced
   parsley
Salt
Pepper
4 medium-size ripe tomatoes
4 hard-boiled eggs
Boston lettuce

Trim beef of as much fat as possible. Cut beef into thin slices. Cut into strips about 1 inch long and ⅛ inch thick. Cut off green part of leeks. Cut off root end, cut leeks in half lengthwise, and wash well to remove any sand. Cut crosswise into 1 inch pieces. Cut lengthwise into ¼ inch strips. Cut onions in half before slicing. Break slices apart to make thin strips. Heat oil in a large saucepan. Add leeks and onions. Sauté, stirring constantly, only until onions are barely tender. Stir in vinegar. Remove from fire. Do not drain. Cut gherkins lengthwise into very thin slices. Cut into thin strips about 1 inch long. Cut potatoes same size as beef. In a mixing bowl combine beef, leeks, onions, potatoes, gherkins, mayonnaise, mustard, shallots, and parsley. Mix well. Add salt and pepper to taste. Add more mayonnaise if desired. Chill. Remove stem ends of tomatoes. Cut each tomato into 4 wedges. Cut each egg lengthwise into 4 wedges. Chill.

❡ Place lettuce on serving platter. Place beef salad in an oblong mound in center. Arrange tomato and egg wedges alternately around salad.

Chicken and Mushroom Salad with Cold Curried Rice

4 cups boiled chicken cut in ½ inch
   dice (meat of 4-pound chicken)
½ pound firm white mushrooms
1 cup French dressing
1 cup diced celery
¼ cup scallions very thinly sliced
1 cup mayonnaise
½ cup chili sauce
½ cup sour cream
1 tablespoon salad oil

½ cup very finely minced onions
1 teaspoon very finely minced garlic
2 teaspoons curry powder
¼ teaspoon saffron crumbled slightly
2¼ cups chicken broth
1 cup long-grained rice
Salt
Pepper
2 ounce jar pimiento strips, chilled
   and drained

Use only caps of mushrooms. (Stems may be saved and used for another purpose.) Cut mushroom caps into ¼ inch cubes. Mix mushrooms and ½ cup French dressing. Chill 1 hour. Peel celery and cut lengthwise. Cut crosswise into ¼ inch dice. Use only white part of scallions. Mix mayonnaise, chili sauce, and sour cream. Drain mushrooms. Combine chicken, mushrooms, celery, scallions, and mayonnaise mixture. Add salt and pepper to taste. Chill. Sauté onions and garlic in oil in a heavy saucepan until onions are yellow but not brown. Stir in curry powder and saffron. Add chicken broth and ½ teaspoon salt. Bring to a boil. Stir in rice. Cover with tight lid and cook without stirring, over lowest possible flame, until rice is tender, 15 to 20 minutes. Cool rice slightly. Stir in remaining ½ cup French dressing. Chill.

❡ Place rice in a salad bowl. Place chicken salad in another bowl. Sprinkle both with pimiento strips.

Chicken, Belgian Endive, and Orange Salad
with Cream Dressing

4 cups boiled diced chicken (meat of
  4-pound chicken)
6 stalks Belgian endive
2 cups shredded iceberg lettuce
4 large seedless California oranges
1 cup thinly sliced celery
½ cup olive oil
2 tablespoons white or red wine
  vinegar

1 teaspoon Dijon mustard
Salt
Pepper
1 medium-size onion, chopped fine
¼ cup heavy sweet cream
1 cup mayonnaise
2 teaspoons lemon juice
2 teaspoons cider vinegar

Remove skin and bones from chicken before dicing. Cut chicken into ½ inch dice. Cut endive crosswise into ½ inch slices. Cut head of lettuce into thinnest possible slices and separate to make shreds. Cut peel and membrane away from oranges, using very sharp French knife. Cut oranges between inner white membrane to make neat segments. Peel celery and cut crosswise into thinnest possible slices. Place endive, lettuce, oranges, and celery in large salad bowl. Chill. Put olive oil, wine vinegar, mustard, ½ teaspoon salt, and ⅛ teaspoon pepper into blender. Put onion into clean kitchen towel or cloth napkin and squeeze onion juice into blender. Run blender at high speed for 15 seconds. Pour over chicken in another bowl. Mix well. Cover with clear plastic wrap. Chill. Beat cream until thick. Fold into mayonnaise. Stir in lemon juice and cider vinegar. Chill.

❡ At serving time place salad bowl with greens on supper table. Drain chicken and add to bowl. Add mayonnaise mixture to bowl. Toss well and season to taste before serving.

Chicken Salad with Cream Cheese Dressing and Broccoli Vinaigrette

4 cups boiled diced chicken (meat of
    4-pound chicken)
4 ounce jar pimientos, drained
2 cups sliced celery
3 ounce package cream cheese
¼ cup light cream
1 cup mayonnaise
1 small onion
2 cans (4 ounces each) mushroom
    pieces and stems, drained

2 pounds broccoli
½ cup olive oil
2 tablespoons red wine vinegar
½ teaspoon Dijon mustard
1 egg yolk
Salt
Pepper
½ cup sliced almonds
1 teaspoon butter

Remove skin and bones from chicken before dicing. Cut chicken and pimientos into ½ inch dice. Peel celery with vegetable peeler. Cut crosswise into ½ inch slices. Cook celery in boiling salted water about 5 minutes, or until semitender. Drain. Stir cream cheese until soft. Slowly stir in cream (an electric mixer may be used for this step). Slowly stir in mayonnaise. Grate onion into cream cheese dressing. Combine chicken, pimientos, celery, mushrooms, and cream cheese dressing. Add salt and pepper to taste. Chill. Remove leaves from broccoli. Peel broccoli stalks with vegetable peeler. Cut large stems lengthwise into pieces that can be served easily. Boil broccoli until tender. Avoid overcooking. Drain. Mix oil, vinegar, mustard, egg yolk, ½ teaspoon salt, and ⅛ teaspoon pepper. Place broccoli in shallow container. Pour olive oil mixture over broccoli and chill. Turn broccoli several times to marinate thoroughly while chilling. Place almonds in shallow pan in oven preheated at 350 degrees. Bake 8 to 10 minutes or until medium brown. Add butter. Toss to coat almonds with butter. Sprinkle with salt.

❡ Drain broccoli and place on serving platter. Spoon chicken salad into an oblong mound on top of broccoli. Sprinkle with almonds.

Lobster and Egg Salad with Beet Dressing

4 live lobsters, 1¼ pounds each, boiled
2 cups diced celery
2 cups diced cucumbers
8 hard-boiled eggs, coarsely chopped
¾ cup raw young small red beets grated
1½ cups sour cream
1 medium-size onion, grated
3 tablespoons cider vinegar
3 tablespoons sugar
Salt
Pepper
½ head iceberg lettuce, shredded
1 cup Chinese cabbage shredded
1 tablespoon very finely minced fresh chives

Cut lobsters in half lengthwise. Remove stomach sac in back of head. Crack claws. Remove lobster meat and cut into ¼ inch dice. Save lobster tomalley and roe, if any, to add to salad. Peel celery. Cut lengthwise in half. Cut crosswise into ¼ inch dice. Peel cucumbers. Cut in half lengthwise. Scoop out and discard seeds. Cut into ¼ inch dice. Place lobster, eggs, celery, and cucumbers in bowl. Chill. Peel beets and grate on metal grater. Mix sour cream, beets, onion, vinegar, and sugar. Add ½ teaspoon salt. Chill. Cut ½ head lettuce into thinnest possible slices. Break slices apart to make shreds. Cut Chinese cabbage crosswise into thinnest possible slices. Toss lettuce, Chinese cabbage, and chives. Place in large salad bowl. Chill.

❡ Combine lobster mixture and beet dressing, blending well. Add salt and pepper to taste. Spoon lobster mixture onto greens in bowl. Toss salad at table just before serving.

Mussel and Shrimp Salad with Tartar Sauce

3 pounds mussels
1 pound shrimp boiled, shelled, and deveined (2 pounds raw shrimp)
1 pound fresh ripe firm tomatoes, coarsely chopped
2 cups sliced celery
1½ cups mayonnaise
¼ cup light cream
1 tablespoon lemon juice
2 tablespoons finely chopped pitted green olives
2 tablespoons finely chopped dill pickles
¼ cup capers in vinegar, drained
1 tablespoon very finely chopped chives
1 tablespoon very finely chopped parsley
Salt
Pepper
Boston lettuce
4 hard-boiled eggs

Remove any leaves and beards from mussels and scrub with vegetable brush under cold running water. Discard mussels that are open. Place mussels in a pot with 1 cup water. Cover pan tightly and steam for 10 minutes. Discard any mussels that have not opened. Remove mussels from shells. Set mussels aside. Lower tomatoes, 1 or 2 at a time, into rapidly boiling water for 20 seconds. Hold under cold running water. Remove skins and stem ends. Cut tomatoes into quarters or sixths and press to remove seeds. Chop tomatoes coarsely and chill. Peel celery with vegetable peeler. Cut lengthwise in half. Cut crosswise into ½ inch slices. Chill. Mix mayonnaise, cream, lemon juice, olives, pickles, capers, chives, and parsley. Add mussels and shrimp. Toss well. Add salt and pepper to taste. Chill.

❑ Drain tomatoes well. Toss tomatoes and celery with mussel mixture. Add salt and pepper to taste. Line a serving platter with lettuce leaves. Place salad in an oblong mound on platter. Cut eggs with egg slicer and arrange slices on salad.

Fresh Salmon and Halibut Salad with Mustard Cream Dressing

1½ pounds fresh salmon steak
    ½ inch thick
1½ pounds fresh halibut steak
    ½ inch thick
1 large onion, sliced
2 pieces celery, sliced
1 small bay leaf
Juice of 2 lemons
Salt
Pepper

2 cups diced celery
12 ounce can artichoke bottoms
3 tablespoons prepared mild mustard
1 small onion, grated
1¼ cups mayonnaise
½ cup heavy sweet cream
Boston lettuce
2 hard-boiled eggs, finely chopped
8 ounce jar pickled baby beets, well
    drained

Pour 6 cups of water into wide saucepan. Add sliced onion, sliced celery, bay leaf, lemon juice, and ½ teaspoon salt. Bring to a boil and simmer 5 minutes. Add salmon and halibut to pan and simmer covered 10 minutes. Let fish cool in own liquid in refrigerator. Lift fish from liquid with skimmer. Discard liquid and vegetables in which fish was cooked. Remove skin and all bones from salmon and halibut, examining salmon carefully to remove stray bones from inside of fish. Break salmon and halibut into large flakes. Peel remaining celery. Cut lengthwise in half. Cut crosswise into ¼ inch dice. Drain artichoke bottoms. Wash in cold water and drain again. Cut into ¼ inch dice. Stir mustard and grated onion into mayonnaise. Beat cream until whipped. Fold cream into mayonnaise. In a large mixing bowl combine fish, diced celery, artichoke bottoms, and mustard dressing. Toss all ingredients thoroughly, adding salt and pepper to taste. Chill.

❧ Line a serving platter with leaves of letture. Arrange salad in an oblong mound on lettuce. Sprinkle with chopped egg. Arrange beets on top.

Cold Artichoke Stuffed with Deviled Crab Salad

8 large fresh artichokes
Lemon juice
1 pound fresh deluxe crab lump or
    2 cans (7¾ ounces each) fancy
    crab meat
¾ cup mayonnaise
½ cup sour cream
1 cup celery chopped very fine
2 teaspoons very finely minced
    parsley
2 teaspoons very finely minced chives

½ teaspoon very finely minced fresh
    tarragon
2 teaspoons Dijon mustard
1 teaspoon bottled sauce diable
1 teaspoon worcestershire sauce
1 teaspoon horseradish
Salt
Pepper
2 hard-boiled eggs, chopped fine
1½ cups French dressing, chilled

Cut stems off artichoke bottoms and immediately rub with lemon juice to prevent discoloration. Remove and discard small leaves at bottom of artichokes. With scissors cut ½ inch off top leaves of artichokes. Rub cut part with lemon juice. Separate leaves slightly from center and with teaspoon scoop out fuzzy choke from center. Sprinkle center with lemon juice. Tie each artichoke with butcher's cord to keep it intact during cooking. Boil artichokes in salted water, to which 2 tablespoons lemon juice have been added, until artichoke bottoms are tender, 20 to 30 minutes. Cool. Remove cords from artichokes. Examine crab meat carefully and remove any cartilage or shell. Mix mayonnaise and sour cream. Combine crab meat with mayonnaise mixture, celery, parsley, chives, tarragon, mustard, sauce diable, worcestershire sauce, and horseradish. Add 1 tablespoon lemon juice or more to taste, and salt and pepper to taste. Slightly separate leaves from center of artichokes and fill cavities with crab salad. Form a mound of crab salad on top. Sprinkle with chopped egg. Chill.

❡ At the table, place a small amount of French dressing at each place for guests to dip artichoke leaves in. Serve artichokes on cold plates.

Shrimp and Banana Salad with Horseradish Dressing

2 pounds cooked shrimp, shelled and deveined (4 pounds raw
   shrimp in shell)
2 cups sliced bananas
1 cup diced celery
4 tablespoons salad oil
2 tablespoons lemon juice
Salt
Pepper
1¼ cups mayonnaise
3 tablespoons horseradish
2 tablespoons heavy cream
1 tablespoon finely minced fresh chives
Boston lettuce
4 hard-boiled eggs
12 large stuffed olives

Bananas should be yellow ripe but not mushy; cut them into ¼ inch slices. Peel celery with vegetable peeler, then cut into ¼ inch dice. Toss shrimp, bananas, and celery with salad oil and lemon juice. Sprinkle with salt and pepper. Chill. In another bowl mix mayonnaise, horseradish, cream, and chives. Cover and chill.

❡ Drain shrimp mixture. Add mayonnaise mixture. Toss well and add salt and pepper to taste. Line a serving platter with leaves of lettuce. Place salad on lettuce. Cut eggs lengthwise into 4 wedges. Arrange eggs around salad. Cut olives in half and arrange on top of salad.

Fresh Salmon and Cucumber Salad with Caper Dressing

3 pounds fresh salmon steak, ½ inch thick
1 large onion, sliced
2 pieces celery, sliced
8 sprigs parsley
Juice of 2 lemons
1 bay leaf
4 medium-size potatoes, boiled and peeled
3 cups diced cucumbers
1 cup mayonnaise
½ cup sour cream
¼ cup heavy cream
2 tablespoons capers in vinegar, drained
1 small onion, grated
1 tablespoon finely minced parsley
Salt
Pepper

Pour 6 cups of water into wide saucepan. Add sliced onion, sliced celery, parsley, lemon juice, bay leaf, and ½ teaspoon salt. Bring to a boil and simmer 5 minutes. Add salmon to pan and simmer covered 10 minutes. Let salmon cool in own liquid in refrigerator. Lift salmon from liquid with skimmer. Discard liquid and vegetables in which salmon was cooked. Remove skin and all bones from salmon. Examine salmon carefully to remove stray bones from inside of fish. Break salmon into large flakes. Cut potatoes into ¼ inch cubes. Peel cucumbers, cut in half lengthwise, scrape out seeds, and cut enough ¼ inch cubes to make 3 cups. In a mixing bowl combine mayonnaise, sour cream, heavy cream, capers, 1 tablespoon vinegar from capers, grated onion, and minced parsley. Mix well. Add salmon, potatoes, cucumbers, and salt and pepper to taste. Arrange salad in oblong mound on serving platter. Chill until serving time. Garnish, if desired, with wedges of hard-boiled egg and ripe tomato.

Ham, Macaroni, and Artichoke Salad

½ pound elbow macaroni, boiled and drained
1 pound mild cured boiled or baked ham, thinly sliced
¼ pound cooked Smithfield ham or prosciutto, very thinly sliced
7 ounce jar artichoke hearts in oil, well drained
¼ pound provolone cheese, sliced thin
1¼ cups mayonnaise
1 medium-size onion, minced very fine
2 tablespoons cider vinegar
½ cup finely minced sweet green peppers
½ cup sweet red or yellow peppers in vinegar, drained and
    finely minced
Salt
Pepper
Boston lettuce
4 large ripe tomatoes
4 hard-boiled eggs

Cut both kinds of ham into julienne strips about 1 inch long and ⅛ inch thick. Cut artichoke hearts in half vertically and then cut into thinnest possible slices. Cut provolone cheese same size as ham. Put mayonnaise in large mixing bowl. Place onion in clean kitchen towel or napkin and squeeze onion juice into mayonnaise. Discard onion. Add vinegar. Mix well. Add macaroni, both kinds of ham, artichoke hearts, cheese, and both kinds of peppers. Toss well. Add more mayonnaise if desired, and salt and pepper to taste. Line a serving platter with leaves of lettuce. Place salad in center of platter in an oblong mound. Remove stem ends of tomatoes. Cut tomatoes into quarter wedges. Cut hard-boiled eggs lengthwise into quarters. Place tomatoes and eggs alternately around salad. Chill until serving time.

Tomatoes with Cheese Salad and Salmon Stuffed Eggs

8 eggs
¼ pound smoked salmon, thinly sliced
¼ cup soft butter or margarine
½ cup mayonnaise
1 cup sour cream
4 tablespoons red caviar
8 firm ripe beefsteak tomatoes large
    enough for stuffing

3 cups diced boiled potatoes
1½ cups diced caraway cheese
1½ cups diced celery
2 tablespoons cider vinegar
1 small onion
1 tablespoon finely minced fresh dill
Salt
Pepper

Boil eggs 15 to 20 minutes. Place in cold water for ½ hour. Remove shells. Cut in half lengthwise. Mash yolks. Cut smoked salmon into smallest possible dice or chop as fine as possible. Mix yolks with salmon, butter or margarine, ¼ cup mayonnaise, and salt and pepper to taste. Pile yolk mixture back into egg whites, forming smooth mounds. Mix ½ cup sour cream with caviar. Spoon sour cream mixture on eggs. Chill. Dip tomatoes into boiling water (1 or 2 at a time) for 20 seconds. Hold under cold running water. Remove skins and stem ends. Cut potatoes, cheese, and celery into ¼ inch dice and place in a mixing bowl. Add ½ cup sour cream, ¼ cup mayonnaise, and cider vinegar. Grate onion into bowl. Add dill. Toss ingredients, adding salt and pepper to taste. Slice each tomato vertically from top to bottom, cutting about three-fourths of the way down, but do not cut all the way through. Again slice in the opposite direction so that tomato forms 4 "petals." Press slightly or cut further if necessary to open petals. Sprinkle with salt and pepper. Fill with cheese salad. Place 2 stuffed egg halves alongside each portion. Chill until serving time.

Cold Asparagus Vinaigrette with Shrimp and Apple Salad

1½ pounds medium-size shrimp
cooked, peeled, and deveined
(3 pounds raw shrimp in shell)
3 pounds fresh jumbo asparagus
½ cup olive oil
1 teaspoon Dijon mustard
½ teaspoon dry mustard
2 tablespoons red or white wine
vinegar
Salt

Pepper
3 cups delicious apples diced
2 tablespoons lemon juice
1 tablespoon sugar
1 cup diced celery
½ cup heavy sweet cream
1 cup mayonnaise
Boston lettuce
½ cup broken walnut meats or
walnut halves

Break or cut off hard white ends of asparagus. Wash well. Peel asparagus below buds with vegetable peeler. Boil asparagus in salted water, using only enough water barely to cover asparagus. Use a large wide saucepan or dutch oven for boiling, and cook until asparagus is just tender, 10 to 15 minutes. Drain well. Chill. Mix oil, both kinds of mustard, vinegar, ½ teaspoon salt, and ⅛ teaspoon pepper in blender. Chill. Peel and core apples and cut into ½ inch dice. Sprinkle with lemon juice and sugar. Chill. Peel celery and cut crosswise into ½ inch dice. Beat cream until whipped. Fold cream into mayonnaise. Combine shrimp, celery, and mayonnaise mixture. Add salt and pepper to taste.

❡ Line a serving platter with lettuce. Arrange asparagus on lettuce, cutting asparagus spears in half crosswise for easier serving if desired. Spoon olive oil mixture over asparagus. Drain apples of any juice and combine with shrimp mixture. Spoon shrimp mixture in an oblong mound over asparagus. Sprinkle with walnut meats.

Avocado Stuffed with Ham, Tongue, and Cheese Salad

4 large ripe avocados
2 lemons
¼ cup French dressing
½ pound cooked corned or smoked tongue, thinly sliced
½ pound boiled or baked ham, thinly sliced
½ pound swiss cheese, thinly sliced
1 cup celery cut julienne
¼ cup red radishes cut julienne

⅓ cup heavy sweet cream
1 cup mayonnaise
1 small onion
1 tablespoon cider vinegar
1 teaspoon sugar
Salt
Pepper
2 heads Boston lettuce
6 ounce package almonds cut julienne
1 teaspoon butter

Cut avocados in half lengthwise. Remove peel, keeping avocados intact. Squeeze juice of lemons over avocados at once. Brush with French dressing. Cut tongue, ham, and cheese into 1 inch strips no more than ⅛ inch thick. Peel celery with vegetable peeler and cut into same size as meat. Cut radishes into very thin slices and cut in ⅛ inch strips. Beat cream until thick. Fold cream into mayonnaise. Grate onion into mayonnaise. Add vinegar and sugar. In large mixing bowl toss tongue, ham, cheese, celery, radishes, and mayonnaise mixture. Add salt and pepper to taste. Pile mixture into avocados, carefully forming a mound on top each avocado. If there is excess stuffing, add it to platter later. Line a large platter with small leaves of Boston lettuce. Place stuffed avocados on lettuce. Chill. Preheat oven at 375 degrees. Place almonds in a shallow pan with butter. Bake 10 minutes or longer, stirring occasionally, until almonds are medium brown. Avoid scorching. Sprinkle almonds with salt. Keep at room temperature until serving time.

❑ Sprinkle almonds over stuffed avocados just before serving.

Cold Avocado with Ham, Mushrooms, and Bamboo Shoots

4 large ripe avocados
Fresh lemons
1 pound boiled or baked ham, very thinly sliced
¼ pound fresh button mushrooms, thinly sliced
5 ounce can bamboo shoots
½ cup thinly sliced cucumbers
½ cup thinly sliced red radishes
1 cup mayonnaise
2 tablespoons heavy sweet cream
1 tablespoon finely chopped fresh mint or 1 teaspoon
  crumbled dried mint
Salt
Pepper
¼ cup sesame seeds, toasted
Boston lettuce

Cut avocados in half lengthwise. Remove peel, keeping avocados intact. Sprinkle generously with lemon juice to prevent discoloration. Cut ham into ½ inch squares. Be sure mushrooms are white and firm. Cut stems and caps separately into very thin slices. Drain bamboo shoots, wash in cold water, again drain well, and cut into ½ inch squares. Peel cucumbers, cut lengthwise into quarters, then cut crosswise into thin slices. In a mixing bowl combine ham, mushrooms, bamboo shoots, radishes, cucumbers, mayonnaise, cream, and mint. Blend well. Add 1 tablespoon lemon juice, and more mayonnaise or lemon juice if desired. Season with salt and pepper. Carefully pile mixture into avocado halves, forming mounds on top. Place sesame seeds in a heavy pan over a moderate flame. Stir constantly until seeds are brown but not scorched. Sprinkle sesame seeds over avocado halves. Line a large platter with lettuce. Carefully lift avocados onto platter. Chill until serving time.

9

~

Pasta and Crepes

THE DIFFERENCE BETWEEN pasta for dinner and pasta for a midnight supper is more than the difference between four and two ounces of spaghetti per serving. Just because pasta is so boundlessly popular in its conventional sauces, it should show a special kind of breeding late at night. It should be imaginatively thought out but not wild. For, no matter whether it appears as Chinese lo mein or Italian lasagna with shrimp, it can never be pretentious.

If the job of boiling and straining a large amount of pasta at the last moment seems forbidding, try cooking the pasta beforehand. Simply boil it *al dente* (to a chewable consistency) or to the stage approaching this. Store it in cold water in the refrigerator. Keep a large pot of water measured on the stove and later, after draining the cold water in which the pasta was stored, cook the pasta until done.

Another device for making it in advance, but not too far in advance—say a half hour or an hour before party time—is to boil the pasta, drain it, mix it with oil or butter, and then store it in a pot above simmering water until it is served. The oil or butter will keep the strands of pasta from sticking together.

To be at its very best, pasta should be freshly boiled as indicated in the recipes below. Actually the job is not so formidable that it takes endless time away from your guests. If you have the pot ready as well as the measured pasta, the salt, strainer, and pasta tongs, the final boiling is simple and the results well worth it.

Spaghetti with Mussels and White Wine Sauce

1 pound very thin spaghetti
5 pounds mussels
1 cup dry white wine
3 cups thick cream sauce (see page 50)
2 tablespoons butter
¼ pound mushrooms, sliced very thin
¼ cup scallions, white and firm part of green, very finely minced
1 tablespoon very finely minced parsley
2 teaspoons very finely minced fresh chives
2 teaspoons lemon juice
Salt
Pepper
Freshly grated parmesan cheese

Wash mussels, discarding any that are open and removing beards and any sea leaves. Scrub mussels well with a stiff vegetable brush. Place mussels in a pot with white wine. Cover pot with tight-fitting lid. Bring to a boil and cook about 10 minutes. Shells should be wide open; discard any mussels that haven't opened. Remove mussels from pot. Remove mussel shells and discard. If necessary, strain liquid in pan through cheesecloth to remove any sand. Stir liquid into cream sauce. Melt butter in saucepan over low flame. Add mushrooms and scallions and sauté about 5 minutes, stirring occasionally. Add cream sauce to mushrooms and simmer 5 minutes. Remove from flame. Stir in mussels, parsley, and chives. Add lemon juice and salt and pepper to taste. Chill.

❡ Reheat sauce over low flame, stirring frequently, or in top of double boiler. Cook spaghetti following directions on package. Place spaghetti on large serving platter or large shallow casserole. Spoon sauce on top. Pass cheese at table.

Spaghetti with Chicken Sauce

1 pound very thin spaghetti
3 whole breasts of chicken, skinned and boned
¼ pound fresh mushrooms
2 medium-size onions
6 tablespoons butter
¾ cup dry white wine
6 tablespoons flour
3 cups hot chicken broth, canned or fresh
Salt
White pepper
Freshly grated nutmeg
2 tablespoons finely minced fresh parsley
Freshly grated parmesan cheese

Cut away gristle from center of chicken breasts. Put chicken, mushrooms, and onions through meat grinder twice, using fine blade. Melt butter in a heavy saucepan over low flame. Add chicken mixture and sauté until chicken loses raw color. Stir frequently, breaking up chicken as much as possible with fork. Add wine and cook until wine is almost evaporated. Stir in flour, blending well. Slowly add chicken broth, stirring well. Simmer slowly 30 minutes over low flame, stirring frequently. Add salt and pepper to taste and a dash of nutmeg. Chill.

❡ Reheat sauce over low flame, stirring frequently, or reheat in top section of double boiler. Cook spaghetti following directions on package. Divide spaghetti among serving plates or place spaghetti on large platter or large shallow casserole. Spoon sauce on top. Sprinkle with parsley. Pass cheese at table.

Spaghetti with Pork and Clam Sauce

1 pound very thin spaghetti
1 dozen hard-shell chowder clams
1 pound ground pork
2 tablespoons olive oil
½ cup very finely minced onions
1 medium-size green pepper, finely minced
1 teaspoon very finely minced garlic
½ teaspoon rubbed sage
16 ounce can tomatoes in tomato puree
6 ounce can tomato paste
Salt
Pepper
Sugar
Freshly grated parmesan cheese

Wash and scrub clams well to remove all sand. Place clams in a pot with ¾ cup cold water. Bring water to a boil. Cover pot and cook until clam shells open wide. Remove clams from shells. Measure 1 cup clam broth and strain through cheese-cloth if necessary to remove sand. Set clam broth aside. Put clams through a meat grinder, using fine blade. Heat oil in a heavy saucepan. Add onions, green pepper, garlic, and sage. Sauté over low flame until onions begin to turn yellow. Add pork. Stir well. Sauté, breaking up meat with fork as much as possible, until meat loses raw color. Add clams. Place tomatoes in blender and blend until smooth. Add tomatoes, tomato paste, and reserved cup of clam broth to saucepan. Add 1 teaspoon salt, ¼ teaspoon pepper, and 1 teaspoon sugar. Stir well. Simmer slowly ½ hour. Correct seasoning if necessary. Chill.

❡ Reheat sauce over low flame, stirring frequently, or reheat in top section of double boiler. Cook spaghetti following directions on package. Place spaghetti in large shallow casserole or platter. Spoon sauce on top. Pass cheese at table.

Spaghetti with Cotto Salami and Eggplant

1 pound very thin spaghetti
½ pound cotto salami or genoa salami, sliced
2 cups diced eggplant
Olive oil
28 ounce can pear-shaped tomatoes
¼ cup finely minced onion
½ teaspoon basil
6 ounce can tomato paste
8 ounce can tomato puree or tomato sauce
1 tablespoon very finely minced fresh parsley
Salt
Pepper
Sugar
Freshly grated parmesan cheese

Cut salami into ¼ inch dice or smaller. Peel eggplant and cut into dice ¼ inch or less. Place eggplant in a saucepan with 2 tablespoons oil. Mix well. Add ½ cup water. Cover pan with tight lid and simmer 5 to 10 minutes, or until eggplant is tender. Drain. Place tomatoes in blender and blend smooth. Heat 2 tablespoons oil in saucepan over low flame. Add onion and basil and sauté only until onion is limp. Add tomatoes, tomato paste, tomato puree, and parsley. Simmer 15 minutes. Add salami and eggplant. Simmer 5 minutes longer. Season to taste with salt, pepper, and sugar. Chill.

❡ Reheat sauce in double boiler or over very low flame. Cook spaghetti following directions on package. Place spaghetti on serving platter or plates. Spoon sauce on top. Pass cheese at table.

Spaghetti with Fresh Tomato Sauce and Prosciutto

1 pound very thin spaghetti
6 pounds fresh, very ripe pear-shaped tomatoes
4 ounces prosciutto ham or Canadian bacon, sliced very thin
¼ cup olive oil
½ cup very finely minced onions
½ teaspoon basil
Salt
Pepper
Sugar
4 tablespoons butter
Freshly grated parmesan cheese

The quality of this sauce depends upon the quality of the tomatoes. If fresh pear-shaped tomatoes (also called egg-shaped or plum-shaped) are unavailable, the summer beefsteak tomatoes may be used, but the usual tasteless winter tomatoes will not do. Lower tomatoes into a large pot of rapidly boiling water, lowering a small batch at a time to keep water boiling. Let tomatoes remain in water ½ minute. Remove from pot with skimmer or slotted spoon. Place tomatoes under cold running water for several minutes. Remove skin and stem ends. Cut tomatoes lengthwise into halves or quarters and squeeze out seeds. Chop tomatoes fine or force through a large colander or food mill. Do not place in blender. Chop prosciutto or Canadian bacon very fine. Heat oil in saucepan. Sauté onions, ham, and basil until onions turn yellow but not brown. Add tomatoes. Cook slowly 30 to 40 minutes until tomatoes are pulpy. If sauce seems watery it may be cooked longer or a few tablespoons tomato paste added. Add salt, pepper, and sugar to taste.

❡ Reheat sauce over low flame or in top of double boiler. Cook spaghetti following directions on package. When spaghetti is drained, return it to cooking pot and add butter. Toss until butter melts. Place spaghetti in large shallow casserole or platter. Spoon sauce on top. Pass cheese at table.

Spaghetti with Veal and Ham Sauce

1 pound very thin spaghetti
½ pound baked or boiled ham, sliced
½ pound lean boneless veal
¼ cup butter
3 slices bacon, chopped fine
½ cup very finely minced onions
¼ cup grated carrot
1 teaspoon very finely minced garlic
¼ pound mushrooms, very finely minced
¼ teaspoon leaf thyme
¼ cup flour
¼ cup dry white wine
3 cups beef or chicken stock
2 tablespoons tomato paste
Salt
Pepper
Freshly grated parmesan cheese

Put ham and veal through meat grinder, using fine blade. Place butter and bacon in saucepan over low flame. Sauté a few minutes or until bacon loses raw color. Add onions, carrot, garlic, mushrooms, and thyme. Sauté until onions turn deep yellow. Add ham and veal and sauté until veal loses raw color. Break meat up as much as possible while sautéing. Stir in flour, blending well. Add wine, beef or chicken stock, and tomato paste. Stir well. Bring to a boil. Reduce flame and simmer slowly ½ hour. Season with salt and pepper. If a thicker sauce is desired, more tomato paste may be added. Chill.

❡ Reheat sauce over low flame or in top of double boiler. Cook spaghetti following directions on package. Place spaghetti in large shallow casserole or platter. Spoon sauce on spaghetti. Sprinkle with parmesan cheese. Pass additional cheese at table.

Chicken and Ham Lo Mein

1 pound very thin spaghetti
1 pound (trimmed weight) boneless
  and skinless chicken breast
½ pound baked ham, very thinly
  sliced
2 eggs, beaten
3 tablespoons peanut oil
1 teaspoon sesame oil
1 teaspoon finely minced garlic
1 teaspoon finely minced fresh ginger
¼ cup very finely minced onion
2½ cups chicken broth, canned or
  fresh

3 tablespoons cornstarch
2 tablespoons soy sauce
2 tablespoons sake or very dry sherry
¼ pound fresh mushrooms, thinly
  sliced
1 cup bean sprouts, fresh or canned,
  drained
1 cup Chinese cabbage very thinly
  sliced
Salt
Pepper

Cut chicken into strips 1 inch long and no more than ¼ inch thick. Cut ham same size. Dip chicken and ham in beaten eggs and drain. Heat peanut oil and sesame oil in large frying pan or wok. Add chicken and ham and stir-fry a few minutes, only until chicken is firm. Add garlic, ginger, and onion and stir-fry ½ minute longer. Add chicken broth and bring to a boil. Dissolve cornstarch in ¼ cup cold water and stir into chicken broth. Add soy sauce and sake. Simmer 2 minutes. Add a dash of pepper and salt if necessary. Chill. Cut mushroom caps into very thin slices. Cut mushroom stems into 1 inch strips no more than ¼ inch thick. Chill mushrooms, bean sprouts, and Chinese cabbage.

❦ Boil spaghetti following directions on package. Reheat chicken mixture in pan over brisk flame. When very hot, add mushrooms, bean sprouts, and Chinese cabbage. Cook 1 to 2 minutes longer, stirring constantly. Combine drained spaghetti and chicken mixture, blending well. Serve in a large shallow casserole with a lid or on a large platter. Pass hot Chinese mustard and duck sauce.

Beef and Green Pepper Lo Mein

1 pound very thin spaghetti
1½ pounds sirloin or porterhouse
   steak
3 tablespoons soy sauce
1 tablespoon cornstarch
3 tablespoons peanut oil
1 teaspoon sesame oil
1 teaspoon very finely minced garlic
1 teaspoon very finely minced fresh
   ginger

¼ teaspoon ground allspice
2½ cups chicken broth, canned or
   fresh
2 tablespoons cornstarch
2 tablespoons sake or very dry sherry
2 large green peppers
¼ pound fresh mushrooms
Salt
Pepper

Trim steak of bone and fat and discard them. Cut steak into strips 1 inch long and no more than ¼ inch thick. Mix 3 tablespoons soy sauce and 1 tablespoon cornstarch to a smooth paste and stir into meat, blending well. Let meat set ½ hour. Heat peanut oil and sesame oil in a large frying pan or wok. Add meat and stir-fry until meat is brown. Add garlic, ginger, and allspice and sauté 1 minute longer, stirring well. Add chicken broth and bring to a boil. Mix 2 tablespoons cornstarch and ¼ cup water to a smooth paste. Stir into pan. Cook 2 minutes longer. Add sake. Add a dash of pepper and salt if necessary. Chill. Cut green peppers into strips 1 inch long and about ¼ inch thick. Cut mushroom caps into very thin slices and mushroom stems same size as green peppers. Set peppers and mushrooms aside and chill.

❡ Boil spaghetti following directions on package. Reheat steak in pan over brisk flame. When very hot, add green peppers and mushrooms. Cook 1 to 2 minutes, stirring constantly. Combine drained spaghetti and steak mixture, blending well. Serve in a large shallow casserole with lid or on a large platter.

Macaroni with Chicken Livers and Water Chestnuts

1 pound elbow macaroni
1 pound chicken livers
Flour
3 tablespoons salad oil
1 teaspoon caraway seeds
½ cup butter (¼ pound)
½ pound fresh mushrooms, thinly
   sliced
¼ cup very finely minced onions
½ teaspoon very finely minced garlic
¼ teaspoon chervil

3 cups hot chicken broth, fresh or
   canned
8 ounce can water chestnuts, drained
   and thinly sliced
2 tablespoons Madeira or medium
   dry sherry
Salt
Pepper
1 cup sour cream
1 tablespoon finely minced fresh parsley

Cut chicken livers in half; if livers are very large cut into thirds. Sprinkle with salt and pepper, dip in flour, and shake to remove excess flour. Heat oil in large skillet and sauté livers till light brown. Set livers aside. Pound caraway seeds in mortar till aroma is pronounced. Melt butter in large saucepan. Add mushrooms, onions, garlic, chervil, and caraway. Sauté, stirring frequently, until mushrooms are tender and mushroom liquid has evaporated. Stir in ½ cup flour, blending well. Slowly stir in hot chicken broth. Bring to a boil. Reduce flame and simmer 5 minutes. Remove from fire. Stir in chicken livers and water chestnuts. Add Madeira and salt and pepper to taste. Chill.

❡ Place sour cream in top of double boiler and heat over simmering water only until cream is warm. Reheat chicken mixture over low flame, stirring frequently, or in top of another double boiler. Cook macaroni following directions on package. Remove chicken livers from fire. Stir in sour cream. Place macaroni in large shallow casserole or platter. Spoon livers over macaroni. Sprinkle with parsley. Serve with grated parmesan cheese if desired.

Noodles with Curried Crab and Egg Sauce

1 pound medium-size egg noodles
2 cans (7¾ ounces each) fancy crab meat
1 cup sliced celery
1 medium-size delicious apple
Fruit juice
3 tablespoons butter
¼ cup very finely minced onion
½ teaspoon very finely minced garlic
2 tablespoons curry powder
2 tablespoons Amontillado sherry
1 quart medium cream sauce (see page 50)
Salt
Pepper
2 hard-boiled eggs, chopped fine
1 teaspoon very finely minced parsley

Examine crab meat very carefully and remove any cartilage or pieces of shell. Peel celery and cut crosswise into thinnest possible slices. Boil celery in salted water until tender. Drain. Peel and core apple and dip into fruit juice to prevent discoloration. Cut apple into slices first and then chop coarsely. Melt butter in a large saucepan over a very low flame. Add apple, onion, and garlic and sauté only until apple is soft. Stir in curry powder, blending well. Stir in sherry. Add cream sauce, crab meat, and celery and bring to a boil. Reduce flame and simmer 5 minutes. Add salt and pepper to taste. Chill.

❆ Reheat crab meat over low flame or in top of double boiler. Add milk if sauce seems too thick. Boil noodles following directions on package. Spread noodles in large shallow casserole or serving platter. Spoon crab meat mixture on top. Combine chopped egg and parsley and sprinkle on top.

Noodles with Paprika Shrimp and Cucumbers

1 pound medium-size noodles
1½ pounds shrimp in shell
1 large onion, sliced
1 piece celery, sliced
1 small bay leaf
2 cups sliced cucumbers
2 tablespoons butter
1 cup onions cut in small dice
1 tablespoon paprika

2 cups thick cream sauce
  (see page 50)
1 teaspoon worcestershire sauce
Salt
Pepper
⅓ cup butter or margarine
1 cup bread crumbs
2 teaspoons very finely minced
  parsley

Wash shrimp. Place in saucepan with cold water to cover. Add ½ teaspoon salt. Slowly bring to a boil. As soon as water boils, turn off flame. Let shrimp remain in pan 10 minutes. Remove shrimp from pan with slotted spoon. Add to liquid in pan the sliced onion, celery, and bay leaf. Peel shrimp; add shells to pan and simmer 20 minutes. Strain liquid and reserve 2 cups. Peel cucumbers and cut in half lengthwise. Remove seeds with spoon. Cut cucumbers crosswise into very thin slices. Cut shrimp diagonally into ½ inch slices. Melt 2 tablespoons butter in large saucepan and sauté 1 cup onions, stirring frequently, until onions are deep yellow. Stir in paprika. Add cream sauce and 2 cups reserved shrimp stock. Bring to a boil. Reduce flame and simmer 5 minutes. Add worcestershire sauce and salt and pepper to taste. Remove pan from flame. Stir in shrimp and cucumbers. Chill. Melt ⅓ cup butter or margarine in small saucepan. Remove from flame. Stir in bread crumbs and parsley. Chill.

❆ Reheat shrimp mixture over low flame or in top of double boiler. Cook noodles following directions on package. Reheat bread crumbs over very low flame, stirring frequently, only until crumbs are warm. Place noodles on shallow large casserole or platter. Spoon shrimp mixture on noodles. Sprinkle bread crumbs on top.

Noodles and Chinese Chicken with Scallions

12 ounces fine-size egg noodles
2 whole chicken breasts (4 halves), skinless and boneless
2 egg whites
M.S.G. seasoning
Salt
Pepper
Soy sauce
¼ cup cornstarch
¼ cup peanut oil
1 teaspoon sesame oil
½ cup scallions, white part and firm part of green, very thinly sliced
5 ounce can water chestnuts, drained and very thinly sliced

Cut each chicken breast in half. Cut away gristle in center of breast. Separate filets from underside of each breast. Flatten chicken with a meat mallet or side of a cleaver. Avoid tearing chicken. Cut chicken with a cleaver or heavy French knife into thinnest possible strips. Beat egg whites, 1 teaspoon M.S.G. seasoning, 1 teaspoon salt, ½ teaspoon soy sauce, and cornstarch until mixture is smooth. Combine chicken and cornstarch mixture. Bring a large pot of water to a rapid boil. Add chicken. Stir well. Cook only until water comes to a second boil, stirring frequently to separate pieces of chicken. Drain chicken. Heat peanut oil and sesame oil in a large skillet or wok. Add chicken. Sauté a few minutes, stirring, only until chicken is heated through. Set aside. Boil noodles until tender, following directions on package. Drain. Mix noodles and chicken. Add scallions and water chestnuts, tossing all ingredients thoroughly. Add salt and pepper to taste. Add soy sauce and M.S.G. seasoning if desired. Chill.

❡ Reheat in top part of double boiler over simmering water. Serve with Chinese mustard.

Lasagna with Shrimp and Crab Meat

¾ pound lasagna
½ pound (cooked weight) shrimp,
　　boiled, peeled, and deveined
　　(1 pound raw shrimp)
7¾ ounce can fancy crab meat
16 ounce can tomatoes
3 tablespoons tomato paste
2 tablespoons olive oil
1 teaspoon very finely minced garlic
¼ teaspoon leaf thyme
¼ teaspoon oregano

1 tablespoon very finely minced
　　parsley
Salt
Pepper
1½ pounds ricotta cheese
1 medium-size onion
¼ pound mozzarella cheese,
　　shredded
Grated parmesan cheese
¼ pound provolone cheese, shredded

Cook lasagna following directions on package. Drain. Cut shrimp in half length-wise. Examine crab flakes carefully and remove any pieces of shell or cartilage. Put tomatoes and tomato paste in blender and blend smooth. In saucepan heat oil over low flame. Add garlic, thyme, oregano, and parsley. Sauté about 1 minute; do not let garlic brown. Add tomato mixture and simmer 20 minutes. Add salt and pepper to taste. Mix shrimp and crab meat with ricotta cheese. Grate onion into ricotta cheese and mix well. Pour ½ cup tomato mixture into large shallow casserole or baking pan. Place half the lasagna in the pan. (Lasagna may be mixed with a little hot water to make it easier to handle.) Place half the ricotta mixture in dollops on the lasagna. Sprinkle with half the mozzarella cheese. Cover with half the tomato mixture. Sprinkle with parmesan cheese. Repeat process but before adding tomato sauce sprinkle top with shredded provolone cheese. Cover with aluminum foil and chill.

❡　Preheat oven at 375 degrees. Bake covered 30 minutes. Remove aluminum foil and bake 10 to 15 minutes longer. Note: If a deeper pan is used, lasagna may be prepared in 3 or 4 layers instead of 2. In this case, allow longer baking time.

Lasagna with Tongue and Ham

¾ pound lasagna
¼ pound cooked tongue, thinly sliced
¼ pound boiled or baked ham, thinly sliced
3 tablespoons olive oil
1 cup very thinly sliced onions
3 cans (8 ounces each) tomato sauce
1 tablespoon very finely minced parsley
¼ pound Bel Paese cheese
¼ pound mozzarella cheese
1½ pounds ricotta cheese
Grated parmesan cheese

Cook lasagna following directions on package. Drain. Cut tongue and ham into very thin strips about 1 inch long and ⅛ inch wide. Heat olive oil in pan and sauté onions until just limp. Combine tongue, ham, tomato sauce, onions, and parsley. Set aside. Shred Bel Paese and mozzarella cheese by forcing cheese through large holes of a metal grater. Grease a very large shallow casserole or 2 medium-size casseroles. Place half the lasagna in the casserole. Place half the ricotta cheese in dollops on the lasagna. Sprinkle half the shredded cheeses in the casserole. Spread half the tomato mixture on top. Repeat process. Sprinkle parmesan cheese on top. Cover with aluminum foil and chill.

❰ Preheat oven at 375 degrees. Bake covered 30 minutes. Remove aluminum foil and bake 10 to 15 minutes longer. Note: If a deeper pan or casserole is used, lasagna may be prepared in 3 or 4 layers instead of 2. In this case, allow longer baking time.

Pasta Shells with Scallops and Oysters Au Gratin

1 pound macaroni seashells (maruzzelli)
1 pound scallops
4 dozen shucked medium to large size oysters
½ cup dry white wine
½ cup water
½ pound mushrooms, thinly sliced
3 tablespoons butter
4 cups medium cream sauce (see page 50)
¼ cup thinly sliced scallions, white and firm part of green
1 tablespoon finely minced fresh parsley
Salt
Pepper
Freshly grated parmesan cheese
2 tablespoons melted butter

Cook macaroni shells following directions on package. Wash scallops. Drain. Place in saucepan with wine, ½ cup water, and ¼ teaspoon salt. Bring liquid to a boil. Cover pan with tight lid and simmer 5 minutes. Drain scallops, reserving liquid. Place oysters in pan with their own liquor and heat only until edges of oysters are curled. Discard oyster liquor. Sauté mushrooms in 3 tablespoons butter until mushrooms are limp. Combine macaroni shells, cream sauce, scallops and their liquid, oysters, and mushrooms together with any liquid in the mushroom pan. Add scallions, parsley, and salt and pepper to taste. Turn mixture into a large shallow casserole. (Use two small shallow casseroles or glass pie plates rather than a deep casserole.) Sprinkle generously with cheese. Chill.

❡ Preheat oven at 375 degrees. Sprinkle two tablespoons melted butter on top cheese. Bake 25 to 30 minutes or until cheese is lightly browned.

Crepes for Stuffing Makes 24 to 28 Crepes

9 whole eggs
4 egg yolks
1½ cups milk
¾ cup water
3 tablespoons melted butter at room temperature
2 cups flour
1 teaspoon salt
1 cup butter

Put whole eggs, egg yolks, milk, water, three tablespoons melted butter, flour, and salt in blender. Blend at high speed until smooth. Stop blender and scrape sides with rubber spatula if necessary to blend dry ingredients. Melt cup of butter over very low flame. Skim foam from top of butter. Very carefully pour off butter so that sediment stays on bottom of pan. The clear butter thus drawn will be used to sauté crepes. Over a low to moderate flame, heat a pan 7 inches across bottom. Pour enough melted butter into the pan to coat bottom. Pour off excess butter. Pour about 3 tablespoons crepe batter into pan with one hand, tilting pan with other hand so that bottom is quickly and lightly coated with batter. If too much batter is poured into pan, crepes will be too thick. If too little batter, crepes will not be proper size. When crepe is light brown on bottom, turn and sauté other side only until it loses raw appearance. Continue to make crepes until all batter is used. Let crepes cool slightly before filling.

Crepes with Ricotta and Spinach

Crepes for stuffing (see page 199)
2½ pounds ricotta cheese
10 ounce package frozen leaf spinach
1 cup onions cut in small dice
2 tablespoons butter
3 eggs
Salt
Pepper
1 pound can tomatoes
1 pound can tomato puree
3 tablespoons tomato paste
2 tablespoons olive oil
1 teaspoon very finely minced garlic
½ teaspoon basil
½ teaspoon oregano
Freshly grated parmesan cheese

Cook spinach following directions on package. Drain well. Press to remove excess liquid. Chop spinach coarsely. Sauté onions in butter until onions are tender. Mix ricotta cheese, spinach, onions, and eggs. Add salt and pepper to taste. Set aside. Put tomatoes in blender and blend smooth. In a saucepan sauté garlic, basil, and oregano in oil over low flame for about a minute. Do not let garlic brown. Add tomatoes, tomato puree, and tomato paste. Simmer 20 minutes. Add salt and pepper to taste. Chill tomato mixture. Place 3 tablespoons ricotta mixture on one end of crepe. Fold crepe on sides and roll up. Place crepe, seam side down, in shallow greased casserole or baking pan. Crepes should be in a single layer in pan. Continue in this manner until all crepes are filled. Chill.

❡ Preheat oven at 375 degrees. Spoon tomato sauce on crepes. Sprinkle with parmesan cheese. Bake 20 minutes. Place under broiler until cheese browns lightly.

Crepes with Ham and Asparagus

Crepes for stuffing (see page 199)
10 ounce package frozen asparagus
¾ pound Virginia style baked ham, very thinly sliced
2½ cups milk
½ cup light cream
¾ cup instant dissolving flour
8 tablespoons butter or margarine
1 medium-size onion, grated
4 tablespoons Madeira or medium dry sherry
Salt
Pepper
Freshly grated nutmeg
2 egg whites
Freshly grated parmesan cheese

Boil asparagus until tender. Drain well. Cut into small dice. Cut ham into tiny squares no larger than ⅛ inch. Put milk and cream in a saucepan with the flour. Stir until flour dissolves. Add butter. Cook over a moderate flame, stirring constantly, until sauce is thick. Simmer 5 minutes. Add ham, asparagus, grated onion, and Madeira. Stir well. Season with salt and pepper and a dash of nutmeg. Store in refrigerator until cold. Place three tablespoons ham mixture on one end of crepe. Fold crepe on sides and roll up. Place crepe, seam side down, in shallow greased casserole or baking pan. Crepes should be in a single layer in pan. Continue in this manner until all crepes are filled.

◖ Preheat oven at 375 degrees. Beat egg whites slightly, just enough so that little bubbles appear. Brush crepes with egg whites. Sprinkle with cheese. Bake 20 minutes. Place under broiler until cheese browns lightly.

Crepes with Clams

Crepes for stuffing (see page 199)
3 cans (8 ounces each) minced clams
¼ cup very finely minced onions
¼ pound fresh mushrooms, cut in small dice
3 tablespoons butter
2 cups milk
½ cup light cream
¼ cup dry white wine
¾ cup instant dissolving flour
6 tablespoons butter or margarine
1 tablespoon very finely minced parsley
Salt
Pepper
2 egg whites
Freshly grated parmesan cheese

Drain clams, reserving juice. Sauté onions and mushrooms in 3 tablespoons butter until onions are tender. If any mushroom liquid remains, cook until liquid evaporates. Set aside. Pour milk, cream, clam juice, and wine into a saucepan. Stir in flour until flour dissolves. Add 6 tablespoons butter or margarine. Cook over a moderate flame, stirring constantly, until sauce is thick. Simmer 5 minutes. Add clams, onion mixture, parsley, and salt and pepper to taste. Store in refrigerator until cold. Place 3 tablespoons clam mixture on one end of crepe. Fold crepe on sides and roll up. Place crepe, seam side down, in shallow greased casserole or baking pan. Crepes should be in a single layer in pan. Continue in this manner until all crepes are filled. Chill.

❡ Preheat oven at 375 degrees. Beat egg whites slightly, just enough so that little bubbles appear. Brush crepes with egg whites. Sprinkle with cheese. Bake 20 minutes. Place under broiler until cheese browns slightly.

10

Main Dish Accompaniments

As THE KNIFE needs the fork and the coffee cup the saucer, so does many a midnight dish need its accompaniment. It's hard to imagine a hot curry without rice or a spicy goulash without noodles. But the dish that plays a supporting role can also be imaginative. Plain noodles, for instance, come to life when they're noodles with sweet peppers in cream. Veal balls in deviled tomato sauce will be noticed with special warmth when they're served with a pilaf of rice and pine nuts. Even a supper dish as routine as hamburgers on buns will be roundly applauded when it's joined by French fried O'Brien potatoes or potatoes parmigiana.

Whether a main dish needs a side dish, and what, is a matter of your own judgment. Naturally you wouldn't serve a potato salad with a main dish of pasta. The age of your guests, their probable appetites, how elaborate you want your table to be are things that only the hostess can know.

Cold salads are often very useful accompaniments. For instance, a busy homemaker will often roast a whole leg of lamb instead of the half leg her family normally consumes, or poach five pounds of fresh salmon instead of a two-pound piece, and then simply chill part of it for serving later. If the sliced cold lamb arrives at the table with a red and white bean salad, or the cold salmon is arranged on a platter with a potato and celery knob salad in Roquefort dressing, the side dish is not just something else to eat but the crowning touch to a supper table.

Rice and Pignoli Pilaf

2 cups long-grained rice
2 ounces shelled pine nuts (pignoli)
4 teaspoons salad oil
¼ cup very finely minced onion
½ cup very finely minced celery
1 bay leaf
1 quart water
2 teaspoons salt

Preheat oven at 350 degrees. Put pine nuts in a shallow pan. Sprinkle with salt and bake 10 to 12 minutes, or until nuts are medium brown. Avoid scorching. Pour oil into saucepan. Add onion, celery, and bay leaf. Sauté, stirring constantly, until onion is light yellow but not brown. Add water and salt. Bring to a boil. Add rice. Stir well. Cover pan with a tight lid. Reduce flame as low as possible and cook without stirring 15 to 20 minutes, or until rice is tender. Stir in pine nuts. Chill.

❡ Reheat over simmering water in a double boiler, adding a little water to rice only if it seems too dry. Stir as little as possible.

Fried Rice with Mushrooms and Smithfield Ham

1½ cups long-grained rice
3 ounce can sliced broiled-in-butter mushrooms, finely minced
4 ounces cooked Smithfield ham or Canadian bacon, sliced very thin
¼ cup shallots or scallions, white part only, finely minced
½ cup water chestnuts finely minced
4 tablespoons peanut oil
2 tablespoons soy sauce
2 eggs, slightly beaten
Salt
Pepper

If possible, rice should be boiled the day before it is served. Drain mushrooms, reserving juice. Add enough water to canned mushroom juice to make 3 cups liquid. Bring to a rapid boil. Add ¾ teaspoon salt. Stir in rice. Reduce flame as low as possible. Cover pan with tight lid and cook without stirring 15 to 20 minutes, or until rice is tender. Chill. Cut ham or Canadian bacon into thinnest possible strips; cut in opposite direction to make very small dice. Mix shallots or scallions, mushrooms, water chestnuts, and ham in a small bowl. Chill.

❡ Break up rice if necessary so that grains do not stick together. Heat oil in a large saucepan or wok. Add mushroom mixture and stir-fry for about ½ minute. Add rice and soy sauce. Continue to stir-fry only until rice is heated through. Add eggs. Continue to stir-fry only until eggs are set. Add salt and pepper to taste.

Harlequin Rice

1½ cups long-grained rice
3 tablespoons butter
½ cup very finely minced onions
1 teaspoon very finely minced garlic
¼ cup very finely minced celery
¼ cup very finely minced green pepper
½ cup very finely minced fresh mushrooms
1 medium-size black truffle, very finely minced
¼ cup very finely minced pimientos
Salt
Pepper

Bring 3 cups water to a rapid boil. Add 1½ teaspoons salt. Stir in rice. Reduce flame as low as possible. Cover pot with tight lid and cook without stirring 15 to 20 minutes, or until rice is tender. Chill slightly. All vegetables that are very finely minced ideally should be no larger than cooked rice grains. Melt butter in a saucepan over a low flame. Add onions, garlic, celery, green pepper, and mushrooms. Add several tablespoons cold water to pan and cook covered only until vegetables are tender. Avoid browning. Combine rice, cooked vegetables, truffle, and pimientos. Toss with two-pronged kitchen fork to blend ingredients. Add salt and pepper to taste. Chill.

❡ Reheat in top part of double boiler over simmering water, again tossing with fork several times while rice is reheating.

Chili Rice

2 cups long-grained rice
16 ounce can tomatoes
¼ cup salad oil
1 cup very finely minced onions
1 teaspoon very finely minced garlic
1 tablespoon chili powder
4 cups chicken broth
1 teaspoon salt
¼ cup vinegar
¼ cup brown sugar

Put tomatoes in blender and blend at low speed 1 minute. Sauté onions and garlic in oil until onions are soft but not brown. Stir in chili powder, tomatoes, chicken broth, salt, vinegar, and brown sugar. Bring to a boil. Add rice. Stir well. Cover pan with tight lid. Cook over very low flame without stirring until rice is tender, 15 to 20 minutes. Chill.

❡ Reheat in double boiler. This is a moist rice dish, and a little stock or tomato juice may be added during reheating if desired.

Rice with Sesame Seeds and Bean Sprouts

1 cup long-grained rice
2 tablespoons peanut oil
½ cup very finely minced onions
¼ cup very finely minced celery
1 teaspoon very finely minced garlic
½ teaspoon salt
3 tablespoons sesame seeds, browned
1 pound can bean sprouts, well drained
1 tablespoon soy sauce

Pour peanut oil into a heavy pot. Add onions, celery, and garlic. Sauté over very low flame, stirring frequently, until vegetables are tender but not brown. Add 2 cups water and salt. Bring to a boil. Add rice and stir well. Cover pot with tight lid and cook over lowest possible flame without stirring until rice is tender, 15 to 20 minutes. To brown sesame seeds, place seeds in a heavy dry pan over a moderate flame. Stir constantly until seeds are medium brown. Wash bean sprouts well in cold water. Drain. When rice is removed from fire add sesame seeds, bean sprouts, and soy sauce. Toss rice with a two-pronged kitchen fork. Chill.

❑ Reheat rice in top section of double boiler over simmering water. Break up rice, or toss if necessary with two-pronged kitchen fork.

Polenta with Apples

2 cups cornmeal
2 cups milk
6 cups water
4 teaspoons salt
2 cups finely diced delicious apples
½ cup butter
1 tablespoon sugar
Freshly grated parmesan cheese

Stir cornmeal and milk in a bowl. Set aside. Pour 6 cups water and salt into the top part of a double boiler. Bring to a boil over a direct flame. Remove from fire. Stir in cornmeal mixture, blending very well with a wire whip. Place cornmeal mixture over simmering water in bottom section of double boiler. Cook, stirring occasionally, ½ hour. Peel and core apples. Cut first into thin slices and then into very small dice. Melt ¼ cup butter in a saucepan. Add apples, sugar, and 2 tablespoons water. Cover pan and sauté only until apples are tender. Avoid scorching. Stir apples into cornmeal mixture. Let mixture cool about ½ hour, or until it holds its shape when removed from pan. Grease a shallow baking pan. Place polenta in small scoopfuls on baking pan; use ice cream scoop holding about ⅓ cup. Melt remaining ¼ cup butter. Brush polenta with butter. Sprinkle with parmesan cheese. Chill.

❧ Preheat oven at 375 degrees. Bake polenta 20 to 25 minutes. Polenta may be placed under broiler briefly for browning if desired.

Polenta Dumplings with Tomato Sauce and Cheese

1½ cups yellow cornmeal
3 cups milk
½ cup butter
1 teaspoon salt
6 eggs, slightly beaten
3 cans (8 ounces each) tomato sauce
¼ cup grated swiss cheese
2 tablespoons grated parmesan cheese

Stir cornmeal into 1½ cups cold milk. In a heavy saucepan bring remaining 1½ cups milk and butter to a boil. Add salt. Reduce flame. Stir in cornmeal. Cook over a moderate flame, stirring constantly, until cornmeal mixture is quite thick. Remove from fire. Slowly stir in eggs until well blended. Cool mixture about ½ hour in refrigerator. In a large wide saucepan or dutch oven bring 2 inches slightly salted water to a boil. Drop cornmeal mixture by rounded table-spoonfuls into water; dip tablespoon into boiling water each time before filling it with cornmeal mixture. Keep portions as uniform as possible. Do not overcrowd pan. Cover pan with a tight lid. Reduce flame and simmer 10 minutes. Handling carefully, lift each piece of polenta from pan with a slotted spoon and place in a shallow container. Drain any water that collects under cooked polenta. Continue to cook remaining polenta in same manner, adding water to pan when necessary. Place polenta in a single layer in a large shallow casserole or baking dish. Spoon tomato sauce over polenta. Sprinkle with both kinds of cheese. Chill.

❦ Preheat oven at 375 degrees. Bake 25 to 30 minutes, or until cheese is lightly browned. Polenta may be placed under broiler briefly to brown cheese just before serving.

Gnocchi with Onions and Peppers

¾ cup farina
2 tablespoons butter
½ cup finely minced onions
½ cup finely minced green peppers
2 ounce jar sliced pimientos, drained and finely minced
3 cups water
1 cup milk
1½ teaspoons salt
2 eggs, yolks and whites separated
Grated parmesan cheese
¼ cup melted butter

Melt 2 tablespoons butter. Add onions and green peppers. Sauté, stirring constantly, only until onions are limp. Add pimientos. Set aside. Pour water and milk into another saucepan. Add salt. Slowly bring to a boil over a low flame. Slowly add farina, stirring with a wire whip. Cook 5 minutes, stirring frequently. Slowly add egg yolks and cook 2 minutes longer, stirring constantly. Beat egg whites until stiff. Add onion mixture to farina. Stir hot farina mixture into beaten egg whites, blending well. Chill in refrigerator until stiff. Using a small ice cream scoop, place scoopfuls of the farina mixture in a well-greased shallow casserole. Sprinkle with parmesan cheese. Again chill.

❡ Preheat oven at 375 degrees. Spoon melted butter over mounds of gnocchi. Bake 20 minutes. If necessary place under broiler until cheese is light brown.

Spaghetti with Onions and Mushrooms

¾ pound very thin spaghetti
½ pound fresh mushrooms
1 quart Spanish onions
1 teaspoon very finely minced garlic
Olive oil
Salt
Pepper
¼ cup grated parmesan cheese
¼ cup grated natural gruyère cheese or Swiss emmentaler cheese

Cut mushrooms into very thin slices. Cut slices into thin julienne strips. Heat 2 tablespoons olive oil in large saucepan and sauté mushrooms slowly until they are soft and no liquid remains in pan. Sprinkle generously with salt and pepper. Set aside. Cut onions in half through stem end. Cut crosswise into the thinnest possible slices. Break slices apart to make thin strips. Heat 3 tablespoons oil in a large saucepan. Sauté onions and garlic, stirring frequently, until onions are light yellow but not brown. Set aside. Break spaghetti into strips about 2 inches long. Boil spaghetti in salted water following directions on package. Drain spaghetti well. In a large bowl toss spaghetti, mushrooms, and onions. The oil adhering to the vegetables should keep the spaghetti from sticking together. However, if the strands seem too cohesive, add a small amount of oil. Add salt and pepper to taste. Chill.

❐ Reheat in top of double boiler over simmering water. Combine parmesan cheese and gruyère cheese. Add to spaghetti. Toss just before serving.

Baked Maccaroncelli with Olive Condite Sauce

¾ pound maccaroncelli
½ jar (12 ounce size) olive condite
3 cups thin cream sauce (see page 50)
2 teaspoons anchovy paste
1 small onion
¼ cup butter
1 cup bread crumbs
¼ cup freshly grated parmesan cheese
Salt
Pepper
Cayenne pepper

Boil maccaroncelli following directions on package. Drain well. Drain olive condite well. Chop fine. Mix cream sauce and anchovy paste, blending well. Add olive condite. Grate onion into sauce. Combine maccaroncelli and sauce. Add salt and pepper to taste and a dash of cayenne. Turn into a shallow large casserole. Do not use a deep casserole. Melt butter in a saucepan. Add crumbs. Sauté, stirring constantly, until crumbs are browned. Combine crumbs and cheese, blending well. Sprinkle mixture over maccaroncelli. Chill.

❡ Preheat oven at 375 degrees. Bake 30 minutes. Casserole may be placed under broiler for additional browning if desired.

Noodles with Sweet Peppers in Cream

¾ pound fine-size egg noodles
1½ cups green peppers sliced very thin
1 cup onions sliced very thin
4 tablespoons butter
½ cup pimientos sliced very thin
¾ cup heavy cream
6 tablespoons grated parmesan cheese
Salt
Pepper

Use the long pale green sweet peppers if possible. Cut peppers in half lengthwise. Remove stem ends, seeds, and inner membranes. Cut into thinnest possible slices. Break onion slices apart to make strips. Sauté green peppers and onions in butter over very low flame, stirring frequently, until peppers are tender. Avoid browning onions. Set aside. Boil noodles until tender following directions on package. Drain. Mix noodles with green pepper mixture, pimientos, cream, and cheese. Add salt and pepper to taste. Chill.

❮ Reheat in top section of double boiler over simmering water, tossing noodles occasionally. A small amount of milk or cream may be added if desired.

Noodles with Ham and Cream

¾ pound fine-size egg noodles
½ cup sliced scallions
¼ pound prosciutto ham, sliced paper thin
½ jar (4 ounce size) roasted peppers
1 cup heavy cream
Salt
Pepper
2 tablespoons sweet butter
½ cup freshly grated parmesan cheese

Trim root ends of scallions. Trim and remove hollow green ends of scallions; firm part of green should remain. Cut scallions in half lengthwise. Cut crosswise into 1 inch sections. Cut lengthwise into thinnest possible julienne strips. Cut ham and peppers into thinnest possible 1 inch strips. Boil noodles following directions on package. Drain well. Add scallions, ham, roasted peppers, and cream to noodles. Toss well, adding salt and pepper to taste. Chill.

❢ Melt butter in top part of double boiler over simmering water. Add noodles and heat, tossing occasionally until ready to serve. Just before serving or at table, add parmesan cheese and toss until well blended.

Potatoes Parmigiana

2½ pounds potatoes
4 tablespoons butter
¼ cup light cream
Milk
Salt
Pepper
2 cans (8 ounces each) tomato sauce
¼ teaspoon oregano
2 tablespoons butter
¼ pound process swiss cheese, shredded
Grated parmesan cheese

Peel and boil potatoes in salted water until tender. Drain. Mash potatoes in ricer or in mixer. Add 4 tablespoons butter. Stir until butter melts. Add cream. Blend well. Add enough milk so that potatoes are moist but not mushy soft. They should be able to hold their shape. Add salt and pepper to taste. With an ice cream scoop that holds about ⅓ cup, put scoopfuls of potatoes on a greased shallow casserole. Scoopfuls should not be too close together. Heat tomato sauce, oregano, and 2 tablespoons butter. Simmer about 5 minutes. Sprinkle swiss cheese over potatoes. Spoon sauce over potatoes. Sprinkle parmesan cheese over sauce, coating sauce generously with cheese. Chill.

❡ Preheat oven at 375 degrees. Bake potatoes 25 to 30 minutes or until cheese is browned. Potatoes may be placed under broiler briefly for browning just before serving.

French Fried O'Brien Potatoes

6 cups Idaho potatoes cut in ½ inch cubes
¼ cup butter
1 cup onions cut in ½ inch dice
1 cup green peppers cut in ½ inch dice
½ cup pimientos cut in ½ inch dice
Salt
Pepper
Deep fat for frying

Peel potatoes. Cut off irregular sides (these may be saved and used for mashed potatoes) and cut potatoes into ½ inch cubes. Try to make cut potatoes of uniform size. Keep potatoes in cold water until needed. Then drain and dry well. Heat clean fresh oil or shortening at least 4 inches deep at 370 degrees. An electric deep fat fryer is ideal for the job. Fry potatoes, a small amount at a time, until only light brown and tender. Melt butter in saucepan over low flame. Add onions and green peppers. Sauté, stirring frequently, until vegetables are tender but not browned. Add pimientos. Season with salt and pepper. Chill in the pan in which vegetables were sautéed.

❡ Heat deep fat at 370 degrees. Fry potatoes (do not overload frying basket) until golden brown. Sprinkle generously with salt. Reheat pepper mixture. Toss potatoes and pepper mixture. Serve on warm platter.

Deviled Potato Balls

2 pounds potatoes in jackets
3 eggs
1 teaspoon salt
¼ teaspoon white pepper
4½ ounce can deviled ham
1 teaspoon worcestershire sauce
¼ cup very finely minced green pepper
1 tablespoon very finely minced parsley
Flour
Bread crumbs
Deep fat for frying

Boil potatoes in jackets until tender. Drain. Peel. Put potatoes through ricer or mash in mixer. Separate whites and yolks of 2 eggs. Reserve whites. Add yolks to mashed potatoes. Stir well. Add salt and pepper, ham, worcestershire sauce, green pepper, and parsley. Blend well. Chill until mixture can be easily handled. Roll potato mixture into balls no larger than 1 inch in diameter. Roll potato balls in flour. Beat 2 egg whites and remaining whole egg. Dip potato balls into beaten eggs, coating thoroughly. Dip into bread crumbs, coating thoroughly. Chill.

❡ Heat deep fat to a depth of at least 4 inches in kettle at 370 degrees. Fry potato balls in several batches until medium brown.

Hot Potato Salad

2½ pounds potatoes in jackets
¼ pound bacon
½ cup salad oil
½ cup onions cut in small dice
½ cup celery cut in small dice
3 tablespoons vinegar
2 tablespoons sugar
1 teaspoon very finely minced parsley
1 tablespoon very finely minced chives
½ teaspoon chervil
½ teaspoon tarragon
Salt
Pepper

Boil unpeeled potatoes until tender. Drain. Peel. Cut into ½ inch cubes. Place bacon in cold pan. Fry over low heat until crisp. Remove bacon from pan. Leave 3 tablespoons bacon fat in pan. Crumble bacon into small pieces. Add oil to pan. Add onions and celery. Sauté until vegetables are barely tender. Remove from fire. Add vinegar, sugar, parsley, chives, chervil, and tarragon. Combine potatoes and onion mixture, tossing well. Add bacon, and salt and pepper to taste. Chill.

❡ Reheat in top part of double boiler over simmering water. If salad seems too dry, more oil and vinegar may be added to taste.

Lima Bean, Apple, and Bacon Salad

1 pound small-size dried lima beans
1 medium-size onion
1 carrot
1 piece celery
1 bay leaf
Salt
Pepper
1 cup chopped delicious apples
¼ pound bacon
¼ cup finely minced onions
1 teaspoon very finely minced garlic
3 tablespoons brown sugar
3 tablespoons vinegar
2 tablespoons salad oil
Salt
Pepper

Wash beans. Place in a pot with onion, carrot, celery, bay leaf, and 1 teaspoon salt. Add cold water to cover about 1 inch above beans. Bring water to a boil. Turn off flame. Let beans remain in water 1 hour. Again bring to a boil. Reduce flame so that water merely simmers and cook until beans are tender, about 1½ to 2 hours. Add water to pot as necessary to keep beans covered. Let beans cool in cooking liquid. Drain well, and discard vegetables and bay leaf from cooking liquid. Peel and core apples before chopping. Fry bacon until crisp. Do not discard bacon fat. Sauté apples, onions, and garlic in bacon fat until onions are yellow but not brown. Remove from fire. Add to beans. Crumble bacon and add to beans. Add sugar, vinegar, and salad oil. Add salt and pepper to taste. Add more sugar or vinegar if desired. Chill well until serving time. Dish is best if made a day before serving.

Rice Salad with Peas

2 cups long-grained rice
¼ cup olive oil
½ cup very finely minced celery
¼ cup very finely minced onion
¼ cup very finely minced green pepper
1 bay leaf
4½ cups boiling water
2 teaspoons salt
6 tablespoons sour gherkins very finely minced
1 tablespoon very finely minced parsley
2 tablespoons tarragon vinegar
1 pound fresh peas or 1 package (10 ounces) frozen peas

Heat olive oil in heavy saucepan. Add celery, onion, green pepper, and bay leaf. Sauté, stirring frequently, only until onion is soft but not yellow. Add rice, boiling water, and salt. Stir well. Cover pan. Cook over very low flame without stirring until rice is tender, 15 to 20 minutes. Stir in gherkins, parsley, and vinegar. Hull peas if fresh and cook in slightly salted water until tender. If frozen peas are used, cook according to directions on package. Drain peas. Add peas to rice. Chill until serving time. If rice seems somewhat dry, add a small amount of olive oil and vinegar to taste.

Potato and Celery Knob Salad with Roquefort Dressing

1 pound potatoes in jackets
1 pound celery knobs (celeriac)
1 cup mayonnaise
¼ cup light cream
2 teaspoons lemon juice
2 tablespoons finely minced parsley
½ cup finely minced watercress
3 ounces Roquefort or blue cheese
¼ cup shallots or scallions, white part only, finely minced
Salt
Pepper

Boil potatoes in jackets until tender. Drain. Peel and cut into thin slices no more than 1 inch in diameter. Remove leaves and root ends from celery knobs. Peel. Boil in salted water until tender, 20 to 30 minutes. Cut into thin slices. Mix mayonnaise, light cream, lemon juice, parsley, and watercress. Mash Roquefort cheese and add to mayonnaise mixture, blending well. Combine potatoes, celery knobs, shallots or scallions, and Roquefort dressing, tossing well. Add salt and pepper to taste. Chill until serving time.

Red and White Bean Salad

1 cup white pea beans
1 cup red kidney beans
2 medium-size onions
2 carrots
2 pieces celery
2 small bay leaves
½ cup olive oil
2 tablespoons white or red wine vinegar
1 teaspoon Dijon mustard
¼ cup shallots or scallions, white part only, finely minced
¼ cup very finely minced pimiento
½ cup very finely minced celery
1 tablespoon very finely minced parsley
1 tablespoon very finely minced chives
1 teaspoon dried chervil
Salt
Pepper

Wash pea beans and kidney beans separately. Place each in a separate pot. To each pot add 1 onion, 1 carrot, 1 piece celery, 1 bay leaf, and ½ teaspoon salt. Add cold water to cover about 1 inch above beans. Bring water to a boil. Turn off flame. Let beans remain in water one hour. Again bring to a boil. Reduce flame so that water merely simmers and cook until beans are tender. Add water to pots as necessary to keep beans covered. Cooking time of beans will vary with their quality and size; check after 1 hour cooking. Let beans cool in cooking liquid. Drain well and discard vegetables and bay leaf from cooking liquid. Beat oil, vinegar, and mustard until smooth. In a mixing bowl combine beans, oil mixture, shallots or scallions, pimiento, minced celery, parsley, chives, and chervil. Add salt and pepper to taste. Add more oil and vinegar if desired. Chill well until serving time. Dish is best if made a day before serving.

11

~

Desserts

WHEN IT COMES to desserts, a supper late at night is usually concluded in the same way as a dinner. A slice of babka at midnight is neither bigger nor smaller than a slice of the same babka served at the family dinner table, or for that matter at an afternoon committee meeting. Actually, the ever-changing variety of ready-to-eat baked goods, both fresh and frozen, as well as the wide choice of mixes, frostings, and sweets of every description, makes it necessary for the party giver to use more judgment than she did in the olden days, when a woman's goal only was to prove that her elaborate Lady Baltimore cake outmatched those of all her friends. Be particularly wary of some of the frozen desserts. A cheesecake that looked so tempting in the frozen food counter may turn out to be so unpleasantly rich that it sticks to the roof of the mouth and has an aftertaste of heaven knows what additives and so-called fresheners. In your local bakery whose quality is generally high, the lemon meringue tarts might be delightful, the lemon layer cake an abomination.

For these reasons it's very important to know the quality of the dessert you're about to buy, or, if you're making it at home, to have made it once and be sure it meets your personal taste. For instance, there's a recipe in this section for a patty of fresh strawberries. A woman these days who makes her own patty shells—a job that takes a fantastic amount of time and attention—does so only if she makes them as a hobby and enjoys spending the time they take. More likely she will buy them. In any event, the patty shells are filled with an easily made cream filling and then topped with sugared, sliced fresh strawberries—not a big production as far as party preparations are concerned. But if the patty shells you've bought are tough, bordering on staleness, or convey the slightest hint of off-flavor or an unpleasant taste of additives, this otherwise pleasant dessert is marred. Obviously the main job here is to find good patty shells. Some imported ones keep their excellent quality even on store shelves; others are mediocre at best. If there's a fine French bakery in your neighborhood, that's the place to get your patty shells—though you may be required to order them in advance.

In the final analysis, the dessert you serve will be enjoyed not for the hours of labor you spent on it but for its own lovely flavor at the table.

Strawberry Lemon Tartlets

8 prepared baked tartlet shells 3½ inches in diameter
1 quart fresh strawberries, stems removed
14 ounce can sweetened condensed milk
½ cup lemon juice
½ cup heavy sweet cream
4 tablespoons apple strawberry jelly

Mix condensed milk and lemon juice. Chill ½ hour. Beat cream until stiff. Fold into milk mixture and chill ½ hour. Spoon into tartlet shells. Beat jelly until soft. Toss strawberries in jelly until strawberries are well coated. Place strawberries on top of lemon filling. Chill until serving time.

Peach Almond Tartlets

8 prepared baked tartlet shells 3½ inches in diameter
8 canned freestone peach halves, well drained
¼ cup sliced almonds
Salt
6 ounce can almond paste
2 egg whites, slightly beaten
¼ cup sugar
1 cup heavy sweet cream
2 tablespoons confectioners' sugar

Preheat oven at 375 degrees. Spread almonds in a small shallow pan and bake 8 to 10 minutes, or until lightly browned. Sprinkle with salt. Work almond paste until it is soft enough to be stirred; if necessary put it through a meat grinder, using fine blade. Slowly stir egg whites into almond paste. Slowly stir in ¼ cup sugar and 2 tablespoons cream until well blended. If mixture is not well blended, force it through a wire strainer. Beat balance of cream until whipped. Stir confectioners' sugar into whipped cream. Fold almond paste mixture into whipped cream. Place peaches, pitted side up, in tartlet shells. Fill with almond mixture. Smooth almond mixture with knife or spatula to make smooth mounds. Sprinkle with almonds. Chill until serving time.

Patty of Fresh Strawberries

8 prepared baked patty shells
2 quarts fresh strawberries
Sugar
1 cup medium cream sauce (see page 50)
1 egg, slightly beaten
1 tablespoon cognac
1 teaspoon vanilla extract
1 cup heavy cream

Slice half the strawberries. Leave balance of strawberries whole. Place sliced and whole strawberries in mixing bowl with ¾ cup sugar. Toss well. Chill. Prepare cream sauce, seasoning it with only ⅛ teaspoon salt. Stir ⅓ cup sugar into hot sauce. Stir a few tablespoons hot sauce into beaten egg. Slowly add egg to sauce in saucepan. Cook 1 minute more over moderate flame, stirring constantly. Remove from fire. Stir in cognac and vanilla extract. Chill. When sauce is cold, beat cream until whipped. Stir 2 tablespoons sugar into whipped cream. Fold half the whipped cream into the cold sauce. Fill insides of patty shells with sauce. Chill. Put caps of patty shells aside. Chill balance of whipped cream.

❦ Place patty shells in serving dishes. Spoon strawberries over patty shells. Spoon whipped cream on patty shells. Place cap of patty shell on top each portion.

Lime Pie with Crême de Menthe

9 inch baked pie shell
14 ounce can sweetened condensed milk
½ cup fresh lime juice
1 teaspoon grated lime rind
3 eggs, whites and yolks separated
3 tablespoons green crême de menthe
Green food color
½ cup heavy sweet cream
2 tablespoons confectioners' sugar
¼ teaspoon peppermint extract

Mix milk, lime juice, and lime rind. Beat egg yolks slightly. Stir into milk mixture. Stir in 2 tablespoons crême de menthe and a few drops green color, blending well. Beat egg whites until stiff. Carefully fold milk mixture into egg whites, using a down, over, and up motion with mixing spoon or spatula, until mixture is carefully blended. Turn into pie shell. Smooth top with spatula. Chill for about an hour. Beat cream until whipped. Stir in 1 tablespoon crême de menthe, confectioners' sugar, peppermint extract, and a few drops green color. Spread whipped cream over pie filling. Chill until serving time.

Spiced Apple Coffee Cake

2 cups all-purpose flour sifted before measuring
3 teaspoons baking powder
½ teaspoon salt
1½ teaspoons cinnamon
¼ teaspoon nutmeg
¾ cup light brown sugar firmly packed
½ cup shortening
¾ cup milk
1 egg, beaten
20 ounce can sliced apples
½ cup brown sugar firmly packed
⅓ cup all-purpose flour
½ teaspoon cinnamon
3 tablespoons butter or margarine
1 tablespoon lemon juice

Preheat oven at 375 degrees. Grease a 10 inch glass pie plate generously with butter. Sift into mixing bowl 2 cups flour, baking powder, salt, 1½ teaspoons cinnamon, and nutmeg. Force ¾ cup light brown sugar through wire sieve into bowl. Add ½ cup shortening. Cut in shortening until particles of shortening are extremely fine. Combine egg and milk. Stir into bowl until no dry ingredients are visible; batter may be coarse looking. Turn batter into pie plate. Drain apples. Arrange apples on batter. Pour ½ cup brown sugar, ⅓ cup flour, and ½ teaspoon cinnamon into small mixing bowl. Mix well. Cut in butter or margarine until finely chopped. Stir in lemon juice. Spread mixture on apples. Bake 30 to 35 minutes.

❦ Before serving, warm coffee cake in a moderate oven for 5 to 8 minutes.

Black Cherry Rum Cake

1 pound can pitted black cherries
3 tablespoons melted butter or margarine
½ cup brown sugar
3 tablespoons dark Jamaica rum
½ cup unsalted butter or margarine
1 ¾ cups self-rising cake flour sifted before measuring
1 cup sugar
⅓ cup milk
1 teaspoon vanilla
2 eggs, unbeaten
⅓ cup milk
2 tablespoons red currant jelly

Use a round 9 inch cake pan 2 inches deep, with nonstick coating if possible. Pan must not be smaller than this. Preheat oven at 350 degrees. Drain cherries well. If cherries are not pitted, remove pits. Grease pan well on sides. Pour melted butter or margarine into pan. Add brown sugar and rum. Stir until sugar dissolves. Spread mixture evenly. Place cherries in pan. Place ½ cup unsalted butter in bowl of electric mixer. Stir until softened. Add flour, sugar, ⅓ cup of the milk, and vanilla. Beat at medium speed 2 minutes. Add eggs and remaining ⅓ cup milk. Beat at medium speed 2 minutes. Pour batter into pan. Bake 50 to 60 minutes, or until top of cake is firm when lightly touched. Do not underbake. Remove from oven. Let stand ½ hour. Invert onto serving plate. Beat jelly until it is syrupy. Spread on cake. Cake may be served either slightly warm or well chilled.

Sherry Cream Cake

½ cup unsalted butter or unsalted
    margarine
2 cups self-rising cake flour sifted
    before measuring
1 cup sugar
⅓ cup milk
1 teaspoon vanilla
2 eggs, unbeaten
⅓ cup milk

¾ cup milk
3 tablespoons instant dissolving flour
¼ cup sugar
⅓ cup cream sherry
⅛ teaspoon salt
2 eggs, slightly beaten
½ cup heavy cream
Confectioners' sugar

Use a 10 inch glass pie plate. Plate must not be smaller than this. Grease plate well. Line bottom of plate with wax paper and grease wax paper. Preheat oven at 350 degrees. Place ½ cup butter or margarine in bowl of electric mixer. Stir until softened. Add 2 cups flour, 1 cup sugar, ⅓ cup milk, and vanilla. Beat at medium speed 2 minutes. Add 2 eggs and ⅓ cup milk. Beat at medium speed 2 minutes. Pour batter into pie plate. Bake 35 to 40 minutes, or until top of cake is firm when lightly touched. Do not underbake. Pour ¾ cup milk into top part of double boiler. Add 3 tablespoons instant dissolving flour. Stir until flour dissolves completely. Stir in ¼ cup sugar, sherry, salt, and 2 slightly beaten eggs. Blend well. Place over simmering water in top part of double boiler. Cook, stirring constantly with wire whip, until mixture is as thick as a pudding. Chill. When mixture is cold, beat cream until whipped. Fold cream into sherry mixture. Remove cake from pan. Place bottom side up on serving plate. Cut horizontally in half with very sharp knife. Spread sherry filling on bottom half. Place top half in position. Sift confectioners' sugar over top. Chill until serving time.

Apricot Ricotta Cake

1 three-quarter-pound loaf sponge cake
30 ounce can whole peeled apricots
1 pound ricotta cheese
½ cup sugar
1 teaspoon vanilla
4 tablespoons cognac
6 tablespoons banana liqueur
6 tablespoons syrup from apricots
½ cup apricot jam

Drain apricots well, reserving 6 tablespoons syrup. Separate apricots into halves and remove pits. Mix ricotta cheese with sugar, vanilla, and cognac, blending well. Set aside. Mix banana liqueur and 6 tablespoons apricot syrup. Chop apricot jam on cutting board until it is a smooth puree. Set aside 2 tablespoons of puree. Cut cake horizontally in half lengthwise. Scoop or cut out enough of the inside of the cake to leave a ½ inch wall, thus making a cake "chest." Sprinkle inside of cake with banana liqueur mixture. Spread inside of cake with the larger portion of apricot puree. Fill with ricotta cheese mixture. Place apricot halves on cheese. Spread apricot halves with remaining apricot puree. Chill until serving time.

Nesselrode Turnovers

Pastry for 9-inch pie
10 ounce jar Nesselro (prepared fruits in rum sauce)
Milk
3 tablespoons instant dissolving flour
⅛ teaspoon salt
2 egg yolks, beaten slightly
1 tablespoon butter or margarine
1 whole egg
Confectioners' sugar

Drain Nesselro in a wire strainer at least 10 minutes, saving syrup that drips off. Add enough milk to syrup to make ¾ cup liquid. Stir in flour and salt until flour dissolves completely. Heat in saucepan over low flame, stirring constantly, until sauce is thick. Stir a tablespoon or two of the sauce into the egg yolks. Add yolks to saucepan and cook about 3 minutes longer, stirring constantly. Remove from fire. Stir in butter until butter dissolves. Add drained Nesselro fruit. Chill well. Preheat oven at 425 degrees. Roll out dough about ⅛ inch thick. Cut into 4 inch squares. (There may be more than 8 squares of dough, depending upon thickness of dough.) Divide chilled filling evenly among the squares of dough. Beat whole egg with 1 tablespoon water. Brush edges of each square with egg. Fold dough to make triangles. Pinch edges shut with fingers or tines of fork. With knife or pastry cutter, trim ragged edges of dough to make straight sides. Brush turnovers with egg. Place turnovers on shallow baking pan or cookie sheet. Bake 20 minutes or until medium brown.

❦ Serve turnovers well chilled or warmed a few minutes in a moderate oven. Just before serving, sprinkle with confectioners' sugar put through fine wire sieve or flour sifter.

Maple Glazed Biscuits a la Mode with Applejack Cream

1 quart vanilla ice cream
8 refrigerated ready-to-bake biscuits
Salad oil
Maple syrup
1 cup heavy cream
3 tablespoons sugar
¼ teaspoon ground cinnamon
3 tablespoons applejack

Cut each biscuit into 6 strips. Place 1 inch oil in electric skillet and preheat at 370 degrees. Fry biscuit strips in small batches until medium brown on both sides. Dip while hot into maple syrup, coating strips thoroughly. Store at room temperature until served. Beat heavy cream until softly whipped. Do not beat too stiff. Fold in sugar, cinnamon, and applejack. Chill.

❡ Place a portion of glazed biscuit strips in each dessert dish. Place a portion of ice cream in dish. Top with whipped cream. Drizzle a small amount of maple syrup on top.

Brandied Peach Pudding

1 cup diced sponge cake or ladyfingers
18 ounce jar brandied peaches
Butter
Milk
4 eggs, slightly beaten
⅓ cup sugar
¼ teaspoon salt
1 teaspoon vanilla extract
¾ cup heavy cream
2 tablespoons orgeat or orzata (almond syrup)

Preheat oven at 375 degrees. Grease 8 custard cups generously with butter. Cut cake or ladyfingers into ¼ inch dice. Drain peaches, reserving juice. Sprinkle 3 tablespoons juice over cake. Add enough milk to balance of juice to make 2 cups liquid. Bring up to the boiling point but do not boil. Cut peaches into ¼ inch dice. In a mixing bowl combine eggs and sugar, beating well. Slowly stir in hot peach juice. Add salt and vanilla. Pour egg mixture into custard cups. Add 1 cup diced peaches and cake to custard cups. Reserve any leftover peaches. Place custard cups in baking pan. Add 1 inch very hot water to pan. Bake 35 to 40 minutes, or until tops of custard are firm when lightly touched. Cool to room temperature. Chill.

❢ Run a paring knife around inside of each custard cup to loosen pudding. Unmold each cup over an individual glass dessert dish or saucer-shaped champagne glass. Beat cream until whipped. Fold in orgeat and any reserved peaches. Spoon whipped cream over puddings.

Blueberry Wine Cream with Meringue

32 prepared miniature meringue shells
1 pint large cultivated blueberries
4 eggs
1 cup sugar
2 cups Sauternes
¼ teaspoon salt
2 teaspoons cornstarch
1 cup heavy sweet cream
2 tablespoons sugar

Beat eggs in top of double boiler. Slowly add 1 cup sugar while beating. Stir in Sauternes and salt, blending well. Cook over boiling water in bottom section of double boiler. Top pan should not be in actual contact with water. Cook, stirring constantly with wire whip, scraping bottom and corners of pan, until mixture begins to thicken. Dissolve cornstarch in 2 tablespoons cold water and add to mixture. Stir constantly until mixture is as thick as a pudding. Remove from fire. Chill completely. Beat cream until whipped. Stir in 2 tablespoons sugar and fold whipped cream into cold wine mixture. Spoon into 8 glass dessert dishes. Place 4 meringues in each dish. Sprinkle blueberries on top.

Coffee Bavarian with Rum Fingers

2 cups double-strength coffee, freshly brewed and hot
2 eggs, yolks and whites separated
Sugar
⅛ teaspoon salt
1 envelope plain gelatin
¼ cup cold water
1 teaspoon vanilla
½ cup heavy cream
1 cup milk
3 tablespoons Jamaica rum
24 ladyfingers
Solid sweet chocolate for shaving

Beat egg yolks well. Slowly add ¼ cup sugar and salt. Soften gelatin in ¼ cup cold water. Stir a few tablespoons coffee into egg yolk mixture. Stir egg yolk mixture into coffee. Cook over a moderate flame, stirring constantly with wire whip, until mixture comes to a boil. Cook one minute longer, stirring constantly. Remove from fire. Stir in gelatin until gelatin dissolves. Stir in vanilla. Cool mixture in refrigerator until it begins to jell but is not set—that is, the mixture is syrupy looking. Beat egg whites until stiff. Slowly add ¼ cup sugar to whites while beating constantly. Fold egg whites into coffee mixture. Beat cream until whipped. Stir 2 tablespoons sugar into cream. Fold cream into coffee mixture. In a small bowl mix milk with rum. Dip ladyfingers about three-fourths of the way into milk until only moistened. Arrange three ladyfingers, dry end protruding, around rim of saucer-shaped champagne glass. Spoon coffee mixture into glass. Continue in this way until 8 glasses are filled. Shave sweet chocolate over top. Chill at least 6 hours before serving.

Cream Almond Meringue

24 prepared miniature meringue shells
2¼ cups sliced peeled almonds
¾ cup sweet butter
¾ cup sugar
4 egg yolks, slightly beaten
1 cup heavy cream

Preheat oven at 375 degrees. Place almonds in a shallow pan and bake 10 to 12 minutes or until lightly toasted. Stir occasionally while baking; avoid scorching. Cool to room temperature. Set aside ¼ cup almonds for later use. Place remainder of almonds in blender and blend as fine as possible in several batches. Cream butter in bowl until soft but not melting. Slowly mix in ¾ cup sugar. Slowly mix in egg yolks, a small amount at a time. Fold in ground almonds. Chill well in refrigerator. Beat cream until whipped. Fold whipped cream into almond mixture. Place 3 meringue shells in each of 8 saucer-shaped champagne glasses or glass dessert dishes. Pile almond mixture in center. Sprinkle with remainder of toasted almonds. Chill until serving time.

12

Supper Drinks

You can be sure that most supper lovers are wine lovers. They may also be whiskey, rum, or ouzo lovers. But whatever their tastes, remember that late at night a noticeable change takes place in most people's manner of drinking. The martinis gulped frenetically at five o'clock to wipe out the pressures of the working day are now forgotten. Your guests will arrive with a wonderful day-is-done feeling, and it's for this relaxed drinking mood that you should prepare. Usually you will offer them a welcome drink upon arrival and another with the food.

When it comes to the specific welcome drink you offer, there are two schools of hosting. The first regularly offers the run of the bar to guests who may wish to pour their own bourbon, Scotch, or brandy, a custom that guests of conservative drinking tastes find comfortable. The second school—with a definitely younger outlook—gets things rolling by passing to everybody the same mixed drink thoughtfully chosen to enhance the party and its food. This one drink may be made from your own individual recipe or a variation on someone else's, may be anything from an exotic rum cooler in the summer to a hot toddy in the winter. A supper crowd with young interests will welcome the occasion to join with others in a communal cup of cheer to which each can react in his or her unique way, like gathering around a freshly built fire, a new tape recording, or a great platter of pasta.

As a general guideline, beer or wine is doubly useful not only as an introductory drink but for serving with supper itself. Mixed drinks are better than

239

straight shots. And light young wines with their effortless glow are better than the great château or estate wines of vintage years with their phenomenally rich after-taste and their even more phenomenally rich price tags. The latter are as out of place at a midnight supper as a teen-ager on his first date arriving in a chauffeur-driven Rolls-Royce.

At a midnight party, no one questions your choice of wine any more than your right to serve hot salmon quenelles or cold salmon and halibut salad would be questioned. What was once a tense problem for hosts—what wine to serve with what food—is now an easygoing hobby. Happily, a late-night supper nowadays usually means a one-dish meal and a single select wine to go with it. Since all supper food is as lighthearted and informal as strolling through the woods, the wine should likewise be a lighthearted one that fills the mouth easily and doesn't set your teeth and tastebuds on edge in your effort to study its anatomy. All over the world, an anything-goes school is drawing in more and more wine drinkers, not because it's the lazy way of doing things but because—defying the old standard of white wine with white flesh and red wine with red meat—a dry red, time and again, turns out to be unexpectedly delicious with a white seafood and a vigorous white magnificent with the red meat of minute steaks garnished with the likes of mushrooms stroganoff.

Large pitchers of iced wine drinks made with fruit juices, fruits, liqueurs, and water or sparkling water may automatically turn off wine snobs, but the younger generations have discovered that wine cups are tart-sweet pleasures with infinite possibilities for variations at midnight gatherings. In fact, a whole nation— Spain—for generations has basked in the sunshine of its great wine cup, sangria, and one of its principal charms is that in Spain no two sangrias are ever exactly alike. The six wine cups that follow are in this delectable easygoing tradition.

Because fruity young wines are inexpensive as a class doesn't mean they are unvarying in quality. Rosés from Portugal, Italy, France, and the United States vary almost as much as the languages of those countries. Sipping them side by side will instantly reveal differences in aromas and flavors, and guide you to the choice of those you consider best.

Any list of wines with foods is by its very nature a poll of the author's biases. Unlike meat, one man's wine is not necessarily another man's poison. A list of wines with foods can be very useful not only in suggesting interesting combinations but in reminding you of good values—wines whose low cost may yield a special return in topping off the evening's fun.

SOUPS, CHOWDERS, SEAFOOD STEWS   Before the soup is served, a medium dry or very dry fino sherry, or a chilled aperitif wine like Dubonnet or Lillet on the rocks, is extremely pleasant. Serving wine with a soup or seafood stew is like mixing a stream with a river; each may be beautiful, but the stream is bound to get lost.

HOT SANDWICHES   California mountain whites or reds, Alsatian or California Sylvaners, or white wines from the Loire—such as Muscadet or Sancerre—as well as all the rosés, are great midnight mates with hot sandwich suppers.

HOT CHEESE DISHES   Although dry white wines frequently are poured into fondue and served with it, ales or beers are the best standbys with welsh rabbit and all other cheese dishes. As a switch from the conventional light dry beers, Guinness stout—either straight or mixed with ale—or the German or Danish dark brews are instant bell ringers.

SEAFOOD   Young Rhine wines and Moselles—or their American counterparts, the Rieslings and Sylvaners—plus the rosés, all well chilled, are perfect for flattering the flavors of any seafood dish in a light sauce. When flavors are piquant or very assertive, as in broiled shrimp oreganata or shrimp in a curried tomato sauce, the California reds like Cabernet Sauvignon, Pinot Noir, or Zinfandel breeze in beautifully.

EGGS   Wine savants usually throw up their hands in despair when they try to match wines with egg dishes. Eggs, they say, are too delicate in flavor, their aromas too fragile, to stand up to any wine with a definite character. This is true of simple dishes like shirred eggs or plain omelettes, but when eggs become hearty supper dishes, they're a different breed altogether. Eggs that, for instance, are garnished with anchovies or sausages in devil sauce fairly beg for wine. Particularly pleasant is the Italian white Soave, a fruity, at times a velvety smooth, wine with its slightly bitter but not unpleasant aftertaste. Equally recommended is the California Chenin Blanc with a hint of sweetness but sufficiently bouncy in flavor to enhance such egg dishes as patty of hard-boiled eggs and finnan haddie.

MEATS AND POULTRY   The French Beaujolais and the American Gamay Beaujolais lead off in this section. The fruitiness and freshness of these young red wines are best brought out when they're slightly chilled. Names like Brouilly, Morgon, and Fleurie indicate different wines from the Beaujolais district in France, and it always pays to do some comparative taste testing if you're buying them in quantity for party purposes. Among whites, the California Sauvignon Blanc and the French non-château white Graves bottled under the labels of prominent shippers are recommended.

COLD DISHES AND SALADS   When wine men argue that no salad with a vinegary dressing is compatible with wine, they usually mean leafy green salads with an oil and vinegar dressing in which the vinegar's sharp flavor stubbornly quarrels with the tartness of the wine's grapes. Cold supper dishes such as salads of lobster, beef, or chicken, however, are of a different order. Here the creamy mayonnaise or cold thick dressing takes the place of the sauce that normally accompanies the same food served hot and coexists happily with wine. Many excellent values can be found among such outstanding red wines as the Rhone valley Chateauneuf du Pape and the California Pinot Noirs or Gamays. Among whites, the California Pinot Chardonnay is always a fragrant accompaniment.

PASTAS AND CREPES (the main-course stuffed variety, not dessert crepes) The association of Italian pasta and Chianti wine in straw-covered bottles is so long-standing as to make many people unhappy when these two do not appear on the table together. Chiantis vary in quality from young rough wines to smooth aged reds—called Chianti Classico, a distinguished aged wine suitable for the most eminent roasts. For late-night suppers, however, the young Chiantis, of somewhat lighter body and with a prickly flavor, are often preferred to their older cousins. Equally happy partners are the California red wines in half-gallon or gallon jugs, estate bottled by the best vineyards, as well as the California Zinfandels and Barberas. If the stuffing with the crepes or the sauce with the pasta is mild and restrained in flavor, a Riesling or dry Sauvignon Blanc will be coolly refreshing.

Rhine Wine Cup   Approximately 2 quarts

48 ounces Rhine wine
2 ounces Grand Marnier
2 ounces Cherry Heering
2 ounces cognac
8 slices cucumber peel, cut 2 inches long and ¼ inch wide
8 ounces chilled club soda

Pour Rhine wine, Grand Marnier, Cherry Heering, and cognac into large pitcher. Add cucumber peel. Chill 1 hour or longer. Just before serving, add club soda and stir gently. Pour over ice cubes into punch cups, wine glasses, or old-fashioned glasses.

8 thin slices lemon

Red Ginger Cup   Approximately 2 quarts

32 ounces dry red wine
12 ounces Stone's ginger wine
4 ounces fresh lemon juice
16 ounces chilled club soda

Pour both kinds of wine and lemon juice into large pitcher. Cut lemon slices in half and add to pitcher. Chill 1 hour or longer. Just before serving, add club soda and stir gently. Pour over ice cubes into punch cups, wine glasses, or old-fashioned glasses.

Mountain White Cup   Approximately 2 quarts

36 ounces California mountain white wine
1½ ounces fresh lemon juice
1½ ounces orgeat or orzata (almond syrup)
8 ounces pineapple juice
8 slices orange
12 ounces chilled club soda

Pour wine, lemon juice, orgeat, and pineapple juice into large pitcher. Cut orange slices in half and add to pitcher. Chill 1 hour or longer. Just before serving, add club soda and stir gently. Pour over ice cubes into punch cups, wine glasses, or old-fashioned glasses.

Rosé Cup   Approximately 2 quarts

30 ounces rosé wine
16 ounces fresh orange juice
4 ounces fresh lemon juice
4 ounces pineapple juice
4 ounces brandy
2 ounces grenadine
2 ounces crême de cassis

Pour all ingredients into large pitcher. Chill 1 hour or longer. Pour over ice cubes into punch cups, wine glasses, or old-fashioned glasses.

Scotch Wine Cup   Approximately 2 quarts

36 ounces Chablis or other dry white wine
4 ounces Drambuie
2 ounces cognac
8 ounces fresh orange juice
8 thin slices fresh very ripe pineapple
10 ounces chilled club soda

Pour wine, Drambuie, cognac, and orange juice into large pitcher. Cut pineapple slices in half and add to pitcher. Chill 1 hour or longer. Just before serving, add club soda and stir gently. Pour over ice cubes into punch cups, wine glasses, or old-fashioned glasses.

Hot Sherry Grog   8 mugs

32 ounces dry cocktail sherry
20 ounces water
2 ounces brandy
4 ounces Benedictine
4 ounces lemon juice
3 tablespoons sugar
8 teaspoons butter
8 pieces stick cinnamon
Whole nutmeg

A comforting late-night drink for friends who've been battered by wintry blasts but don't want to be battered by too much alcohol. Pour sherry, water, brandy, Benedictine, lemon juice, and sugar into a large saucepan. Stir to dissolve sugar. Heat very slowly. As soon as grog shows first signs of boiling, turn off flame. Pour into mugs. Add one teaspoon butter and one piece of stick cinnamon to each mug. Grate nutmeg over each drink.

Index